TABLE OF CONTENTS

Top 20 Test Taking Tips

1. Carefully follow all the test registration procedures

2. Know the test directions, duration, topics, question types, how many questions

3. Setup a flexible study schedule at least 3-4 weeks before test day

4. Study during the time of day you are most alert, relaxed, and stress free

5. Maximize your learning style; visual learner use visual study aids, auditory learner use auditory study aids

6. Focus on your weakest knowledge base

7. Find a study partner to review with and help clarify questions

8. Practice, practice, practice

9. Get a good night's sleep; don't try to cram the night before the test

10. Eat a well balanced meal

11. Know the exact physical location of the testing site; drive the route to the site prior to test day

12. Bring a set of ear plugs; the testing center could be noisy

13. Wear comfortable, loose fitting, layered clothing to the testing center; prepare for it to be either cold or hot during the test

14. Bring at least 2 current forms of ID to the testing center

15. Arrive to the test early; be prepared to wait and be patient

16. Eliminate the obviously wrong answer choices, then guess the first remaining choice

17. Pace yourself; don't rush, but keep working and move on if you get stuck

18. Maintain a positive attitude even if the test is going poorly

19. Keep your first answer unless you are positive it is wrong

20. Check your work, don't make a careless mistake

Scientific Considerations

Integumentary system

The integumentary system encompasses the skin and its structural components and layers as well as the additional organs associated with the skin. The skin itself consists of several outer layers collectively known as the epidermis; stratums of the dermis below those; and a whole network of glands, nerve endings, blood vessels, lymph glands, and other tissues beneath those layers. The outer portions are also known as the stratified epithelium because they are somewhat layered and they basically consist of dead cells that act as protective barriers to the outside. The cells of the dermis, on the other hand, are living and are comprised of thick, tough connective tissue. The bottom layer with all its interconnecting glands and other tissues is often referred to as the subcutaneous layer.

Epidermis

Upper layers

The epidermal layers of the skin contain a protein called keratin which protects the outermost portions from external assault. This occurs because as the living dermal cells travel upwards through the epidermis, they divide, eventually die, and acquire this protein undergoing a process called keratinization. There are essentially two sections of the epidermis. The top section, known as the horny zone, actually has three sublayers. The thickest and outer part is the stratum corneum where these dead cells are continuously lost. The middle portion of the horny zone, termed the stratum lucidum, is really only observed in areas such as the palm where the epidermis is unusually thick. Both of these layers contain non-nucleated cells. Skin is opaque because in the next layer, the stratum granulosum, there are live, nucleated cells with particles containing keratin.

Lower layers

Below the stratum granulose is a section called the germinal zone, which is further subdivided into two stratums, the spinosum and the germinativum. The latter (and also the deepest) layer is where cells divide and produce fresh epidermis. The stratum germinativum is also where cells that produce the pigment melanin (melanocytes) are located; these cells influence skin pigmentation and protect against harmful sun injury. Sometimes the germinativum and its single-celled upper layer, the stratum mucosum are referred to collectively as the malpighian.

Dermis

The dermis consists of two layers, both with living cells and each containing the fibrous connective tissue collagen. Right underneath the epidermis is the papillary layer. The main functions of the papillary layer are (1) to provide a bond to the epidermis by extending protuberances called papillae into the latter, (2) to enclose the hair sacs, and (3) to facilitate the sense of touch via nerve endings. Below this area is a quite broad portion called the reticular layer which serves as a conduit for a variety of glands and vessels and connects to the underlying subcutaneous or adipose tissue with high fat content. Blood vessels in the area provide oxygen and nourishment, while lymph glands carry wastes away. Nerve fibers in the reticular layer transport messages to the brain such as presence of pain.

Glands

There are also two types of glands found in the dermal layer, the sudoriferous or sweat glands, and the oil-producing or sebaceous glands. There are two types of sudoriferous glands, both regulated by the sympathetic nervous system. Throughout the body, water-based sweat is expelled through the eccrine glands, but there are also other kinds of glands termed apocrine located in areas of excessive hair such as the armpit. Here the body can smell unsightly because the sweat has interacted with local waste products and bacteria. The sebaceous glands secrete sebum, and they are more concentrated in the facial and scalp areas.

Pilosebaceous unit

A pilosebaceous unit is the complete entity that contains the hair and surrounding attachments. Hair essentially protrudes from the skin surface into the follicular canal. This means that the various skin layers are basically pushed into this hair follicle as well. The terminus of the hair shaft that is formed extends into the subcutaneous layer into what is

Copyright © Mometrix Media. You have been licensed one copy of this document for personal use only. Any other reproduction or redistribution is strictly prohibited. All rights reserved.

termed the hair follicle bulb. This latter bulb is the region where hair actually grows from. The parts of the hair below the skin surface are referred to as the root and they are covered by two layers of root sheaths, the inner part with keratinized cells and an outer extension of the epidermal cells. The attached papillary layer of the dermis provides nourishment from the vascular system and oil to lubricate the hair via the sebaceous gland. There is also a muscle connected to the hair shaft called the arrector pili which controls the temperature of the skin surface by raising the hair and pulling a layer of air under the skin's exterior.

Hair

The hair itself is usually composed of three layers. The cells found in each layer are different. The most central part of the hair is called the medulla. The medulla consists of disc-shaped cells and is more prevalent in individuals with wavy hair; it may be absent in people with fine hair. External to the medulla is the cortex of the hair which is the portion that dictates the color of the hair because it contains melanin. The cells of the cortex are more drawn out in shape; they also strengthen and provide suppleness to the hair. There is also a clear protective layer covering the other hair parts called the cuticle. The cells here are scaly and translucent in appearance.

Types

There are primarily three kinds of hair, only two of which are found in adults. Before or shortly after birth, a baby is covered with a very fine, possibly colored, type of hair called lanugo or fetal hair. This hair is discarded within a few weeks. When permanent hair grows in, it becomes one of two types depending on the texture and distribution. One type of permanent hair is called vellus; this kind has no color, lacks a medulla, and is very fine. Vellus hair is primarily observed in the facial area of females. On the other hand, terminal hair is much rougher and longer and does contain pigmentation. Both sexes have this type of hair on their heads and extremities as well as in groin and armpit areas after becoming sexually mature. In men, terminal hair is also present in the facial area as well as possibly the chest and back.

<u>Stages of growth</u>

Hair basically goes through three stages of proliferation. In the first phase, hair is actively growing and lengthening; this is known as the anagen. The majority of hair on the scalp and face is in the anagen phase and can remain there for up to eight years on the head. If the hair shaft is damaged in this phase, it is said to be dystrophic and a number of hair diseases can result. There is a transitional stage where the hair follicle shrivels in size and begins to separate from the surrounding structures. This phase is called the catagen and is very short-lived. Contraction and separation continues to occur until the hair reaches the final resting or telogen phase. The majority of body hair as well as the eyebrow and ear hairs are generally in this phase. Eventually the old hair is extruded from the follicle and a new hair begins to grow there starting another anagen phase.

The number of hair follicles is similar in both sexes and never increases after birth. The quantity of growing hair is therefore dependent upon the activity of the hair follicles, which is stimulated by androgens or pharmacologic agents. A large proportion of hair follicles lie dormant until they are stimulated to grow hair. If hair in the resting telogen phase is removed by external measures instead of being naturally shed, hair from that follicle will only become observable when new growing anagen phase hair appears. New anagen hair can emerge within a few days after shaving or using depilatories, but it will not be observed after partial electrolysis, plucking, or waxing until at least 2 months after the procedure.

Skin

One of the major functions of the skin is to prevent penetration of the plentiful bacteria found on its exterior. This is primarily accomplished because sweat and therefore the skin surface are both usually acidic, with a pH in the 5 to 5.7 range. The only areas where bacteria can usually thrive are the groin and armpits where people perspire quite a bit and the skin is suppler. If the skin is penetrated by invading microorganisms, immunologic and inflammatory mechanisms are activated; a type of cell in the epidermis called the Langerhans' cell identifies the bacteria or other organism and signals the leucocytes to begin an immune cascade to engulf and destroy the invader. Oily secretions or sebum are secreted by the sudoriferous glands and are found on the surface of the skin; they not only make it somewhat impervious to liquids but also appear to kill fungi. In addition, the skin thwarts loss of important bodily fluids. The melanocytes containing pigmentation shield against UV sun damage, and the fat tissue found in the subcutaneous layer protects against impacts.

Regulating body temperature

There are several ways in which the skin is involved in regulating body temperature. The most important way is that when an individual perspires because they are hot, this sweat disperses into the air and the skin is cooled off. If the person is too cold, perspiration is prevented. In addition, the narrowest blood vessels called the capillaries found in the area respond to temperature changes. If the individual is too hot, the capillaries will widen or dilate to dissipate the heat. Conversely, these vessels will narrow or constrict when a person is cold enabling them to retain heat. Insulation and temperature regulation are provided in two other ways: (1) the oily secretions prevent hair from breaking and falling out, and (2) subcutaneous fat tissue pads and provides an insulating effect.

Cosmeceuticals

Cosmeceuticals are topical ointments of some type that are prescribed by a healthcare professional such as a dermatologist. They are usually given because they are more effective in treating skin disorders. Normally, the skin with its oily properties prevents water-based products from being absorbed. While most cosmetics available without prescription do not significantly alter the absorption properties of the skin, these cosmeceuticals may change these traits. Thus the cosmeceutical may be able to penetrate the skin barriers and be taken into the vascular system. Thus, use of these agents must be closely monitored by the individual and their physician.

Skin lesions

When the skin's structure has been altered due to either some traumatic event or an infectious or immunologic disease, a skin lesion is formed. Less severe or primary skin lesions can range from simple discoloration such as freckling to a variety of types of swelling filled with water, pus, or some type of solid material. Later in the disease process, secondary lesions can develop usually because substances have accumulated on the skin or the surface has actually been eroded. Some skin lesions are termed tertiary if blood vessels are involved and have broken into the area and are characterized by red spots or blotches on the skin surface. Skin diseases are usually treated by dermatologists or sometimes allergists.

Primary lesions

Primary lesions that are merely surface discolorations are called macules and can be either tiny spots or larger patches of skin. Many primary lesions are elevated however. Some of these raised areas are due to some type of fluid build-up. If that fluid is clear, the lesion is called either a vesicle or a bulla depending on the size of the elevation or blister, with a bulla being the larger of the two. If the raised area contains pus, it is termed a pustule. Primary lesions that are raised and solid to the touch fall into a variety of categories. Depending on the size, palpable raised areas could are termed papules, plaques, or nodules with the latter being the largest. These are somewhat regular in shape, whereas another type called a tumor fluctuates more in form. Raised lesions that itch and swell are temporary in nature, are generally referred to as wheals, and typically present after some type of bite or allergic reaction.

Secondary skin lesions

Some secondary skin lesions occur on the surface of the skin. Two kinds falling into this category involve surface accretion of either epidermis (scale or dandruff) or a combination of blood components, pus, and possible epidermis as well (crust or scab). Keloid scars, which are slightly raised discolored scars resulting from dermal restoration, are possible surface phenomenon too. Many secondary lesions involve degradation of the skin surface. These include relatively superficial erosion of the epidermis, excoriation or sores resulting from rubbing the primary lesion, cracks or fissures that extend to the dermal layers, or larger deep ulcers that usually contain pus.

Skin diseases

Bacterial

Skin diseases involving infectious agents can be due to not only bacteria but also to fungi, parasites, or viruses. Bacterial infections are highly contagious and can spread to the circulation resulting in a condition called septicemia. Therefore, it is important to identify these skin lesions and treat them with topical or systemic antibiotics. A lesion that is bacterial in origin contains pus. The most common agents are either streptococci or staphylococci. If the lesion is dark and crusty, it is called impetigo. If the manifestation is a painful, encapsulated pustule, then the lesion is called an abscess. In the latter case, dead cells form in the center of the capsule as a result of some intrusion such as a piece of wood and the capsule forms around it.

Viral skin infections

Viruses are very small particles with genetic material and a covering. They use other organisms to multiply. A cold sore is usually caused by the virus herpes simplex type 1. This virus remains quiescent in the body until stressful, hormonal, or some other external event precipitates a break out. Then fluid-filled blisters typically develop in the mouth region. Warts are caused by viruses as well. One type of wart, verucca vulgaris, is usually found on hands (mostly on the digits) and is characterized by raised areas of cells containing keratin. Another kind of wart called verucca plantaris is observed on the bottom of the foot. In this case, the infection digs a hole into the foot. Both of these types of warts may need to be removed by a doctor.

Fungal and parasitic infections

A fungus is a spore-producing microorganism that lives off other organic matter, in this case the human skin cells. The infections that these fungi cause are generally termed mycoses. They are usually less easily spread than bacterial infections, but also harder to treat and require special medications. The most common type of fungal infection affecting the skin is ringworm, also known as tinea corporis, characterized by somewhat round red patches of skin. The disease is very contagious because people tend to rub the lesions spread the infection. Parasites attach to other organisms in order to grow as well. The most common type of skin parasitic infection is pediculosis in which lice live off human blood and multiply in many body areas, most commonly the head or pubic areas. There are a number of available topical treatments for this disease but it is difficult to identify visually.

Immunologic

Immunologic reactions can cause two types of skin diseases, either allergic reactions or autoimmune diseases. Skin diseases that are allergy-based occur because some agent recognized as foreign is applied to the skin, eaten, or inhaled. IgE type antibodies are elicited against the agents and histamine is released from a type of cell called the mast cell. Allergens can cause systemic reactions as well, including the potentially fatal anaphylaxis. Allergic reactions present on the skin as either urticaria or eczema. Urticaria or hives is a skin condition characterized by itchy swollen lesions. Eczema is itchy as well but the skin tends to flake off. Autoimmune diseases occur because the body does not recognize some its own cells as self and forms antibodies against its own components. Inflammation occurs as a result. There are a number of autoimmune diseases, generally with some systemic involvement, but the most common skin disorder is a variation of lupus erythematosus. Lupus can cause a skin version called discoid lupus erythematosus in which inflamed hair follicles form boils or red patches, primarily in the upper torso and extremities.

Chemicals reactions

External contact with chemicals in products like hair dyes or perfumes or metallic content of jewelry are a few ways people are exposed to potential skin reactions. If an allergic individual ingests certain foods or drugs, they can develop systemic and/or skin reactions. People often develop allergies to antibiotics like penicillin or erythromycin. Some individuals develop small raised bumps on their skin if they are hypersensitive to ultraviolet irradiation. Some plants exude thick organic resins, including poison oak and poison ivy. If an individual is exposed to these resins, they can break out with contagious lesions that are itchy and raised.

Hormonal changes

Hormonal changes occur at various times of life. While they affect the whole body, these changes can manifest as certain skin diseases. The most common hormonal-induced skin problem is some variant of acne. The variant whose onset is generally adolescence is termed acne vulgaris, and it is triggered by overactive sebaceous glands. The facial (and occasionally chest or back) skin lesions present in a variety of forms. Masses of keratinized cells are either some type of whitehead or blackhead (oxidation of the keratin). Some of the lesions become infected and contain pus as well. Another variant called acne rosacea emerges in some women in adulthood. Again, hormonal changes are thought to play a role. In this case, capillaries in the face either rupture or dilate and cause redness. Breakouts can be precipitated by stressful situations, some foods, and extremes in weather. Overactive sebaceous glands can also cause dandruff or seborrhea. Another condition called psoriasis

- 12 -

is felt to be hormonal-induced; the disease presents with red areas superimposed with white scaly sections.

Skin cancer

Skin cancer or carcinoma is for the most part caused by exposure to ultraviolet irradiation. Cancer is the uncontrolled multiplication of abnormal cells in the body. The most widespread form of skin cancer is basal cell carcinoma. This form usually occurs in light-skinned individuals with previous sunburns, and it is usually is confined to the site. Squamous cell carcinoma presents as dark, jagged, scaly skin areas; this form is more likely to metastasize or spread but if recognized easily treatable. The most harmful type of skin carcinoma is melanoma, in which the cells that produce the dark pigment melanin begin to grow uncontrollably. These melanocytes begin to spread to other areas much earlier than other forms of skin cancer. Melanoma can be visually screened for by observing that these lesions are asymmetrical, have irregular borders and color variations, are usually greater than 6mm in diameter, and have increased in size over time.

Glands

Glands are cell masses or organs that either secrete chemicals into or remove them from the bloodstream or lymphatic system. Exocrine glands are generally small channels that either carry substances to needed areas or aid in the elimination of waste materials. These substances include enzymes that catalyze chemical reactions, sebum, mammary milk, and other compounds. On the other hand, endocrine glands produce substances called hormones that either regulate or stimulate a number of systems in the body. These hormones are released directly into the vascular system from the endocrine glands and serve to modulate other hormones positively or negatively as well. Some of the endocrine glands are involved in the stimulation of hair growth.

Glands found in the brain

The part of the brain called the hypothalamus controls the involuntary tasks of the body including the release of hormones, but it is not technically a gland or a direct component of the endocrine system. The chief gland found in the brain is the pituitary gland. The pituitary secretes an array of hormones, and it is divided into two lobes, the neurohypophysis or back region and the adenohypophysis located in the anterior or frontal portion. The majority of the pituitary hormones are secreted from the latter region. There is also another gland in the brain called the pineal gland which releases melatonin, a hormone that controls cyclical physiological changes like sleep and waking.

Pituitary gland

Many of the hormones that are secreted by the pituitary gland are related to sexual or reproductive functions. These hormones include several released from the frontal adenohypophysis area such as adrenocorticotropic hormone, follicle stimulating hormone, luteinizing hormone, and lactogenic hormone. The posterior region produces another hormone called oxytocin that controls muscles in the uterus and nipples in a woman when she gives birth or lactates respectively. The frontal portion also secretes growth hormone, the thyrotrophic hormone that sequentially controls the thyroid gland (which itself affects growth and metabolism), and the hormone that controls skin pigmentation called the melanocyte stimulating hormone. An important hormone released by the neurohypophysis region is the antidiuretic hormone which controls the concentration of fluid in the vascular system and urine.

Endocrine glands

One of the most important glands is found in the neck region, the thyroid gland. It surrounds the windpipe and voice box areas. The hormones secreted by the thyroid gland contain iodine, which needs to be maintained at a certain level. The major chemical released from this gland is called thyroxine, and it is important because it regulates a number of life-sustaining activities including blood pressure and heart rate. There are relatively smaller structures called the parathyroid glands entrenched within the thyroid gland that regulate calcium concentrations in a number of systems. The major gland in the chest region is the thymus, which is primarily involved in early growth of cells and tissues related to the immune system through production of the hormone thymosin. The thymus also generates a growth-stimulating hormone called promine.

There are two types of what are called adrenal glands in the abdominal region directly above the kidneys. The term "adrenal" means that they are related to the kidney. The cortex portion of these glands produces dozens of different hormones that are called

- 14 -

steroids, which are fat-soluble organic compounds with carbon ring structures. Some of these steroid hormones regulate mineral concentrations and thus electrolyte and fluid balance (mineralcorticoids), glucose and or certain pituitary hormone levels (glucocorticoids), or some sexual functions (sex steroids). On the other hand, the medulla region of the adrenal glands really only produces two very important substances: (1) epinephrine, whose major function is to aid in the catabolism of liver glycogen and (2) norepinephrine, which constricts blood vessels. Near the pancreas, there are other glands called the islets of Langerhans that release hormones that control blood sugar concentrations. Insulin depresses sugar levels while glucagons raise them.

Female hormones

The female sex steroids estrogen (and the estradiol form of it) and progesterone are produced in the ovaries, which are located in the groin area of a woman. Estrogens are primarily responsible for the maturity of female secondary sexual characteristics including development of sexual organs, fat distribution, and growth of hair in the area. Progesterone, along with estrogen, enables development of a fertilized egg in the womb by thickening the uterine lining. Other hormones stimulated by the hypothalamus or pituitary gland are involved in various stimulatory and feedback mechanisms as well. In particular, luteinizing hormone stimulates the ovary's follicle called the corpus luteum to develop and secrete these sex steroids during the menstrual cycle. To a much lesser extent, the male sex steroid androgen is also secreted from this area.

Male reproductive system

Androgens, primarily testosterone, are the main hormones produced by the male sexual organs. They are often referred to as anabolic steroids because in addition to the roles they serve in sexual development (such as male pattern hair development and voice lowering), they also stimulate protein synthesis. In the testes of the male, luteinizing hormone stimulates testosterone release from unique cells called Leydig cells in the interstitial tissue. In another part of the testicle called the somniferous tubules, follicle stimulating hormone induces sperm formation for female egg fertilization. Small amounts of estrogen and progesterone are produced in the male as well.

- 15 -

Hypertrichosis and hirsutism

Hypertrichosis and hirsutism are both conditions where there is a perception of excess hair in unusual areas of the body. Both conditions usually involve terminal hair growth patterns. In hirsutism, male androgens are actually overstimulated during puberty in a female, and the woman therefore develops a hair distribution pattern similar to an adult male and possibly menstrual or fertility problems. Pharmacologic agents and endocrine abnormalities can cause hirsutism. On the other hand, hypertrichosis is characterized by some excessive hair growth on parts of the body but not in an adult male arrangement. Many life changes can precipitate hypertrichosis, including menopause, oncology procedures, and medical treatments or actions. Various ethnic groups have somewhat different hair patterns that may be termed hypertrichosis because the condition and what is considered acceptable is actually very subjective.

Hormonal disorders

There are several disorders resulting from hormonal imbalances that present with hirsutism, or male pattern hair distribution, in conjunction with other symptoms. In all of these disorders, androgens are overproduced. One of these syndromes is acromegaly, in which too much growth hormone is produced; in addition to hirsuitism, this causes distended bones, enlarged features or bone structure, and possible vision problems. If the adrenal cortex does not function properly and cortisol is not produced, a condition called virilism or adrenogenital syndrome can result; here again, excessive amounts of androgens are synthesized and the consequences can include not only hirsuitism but also secondary characteristics such as a deep voice and enlarged clitoris. If the adrenal glands produce too much androgens or other hormones, abnormally high blood sugar levels or hyperglycemia can result in a group of symptoms called Cushing's syndrome; other signs are cessation of menstruation, distended and weakened areas in the trunk of the body but not the extremities, and male pattern hair growth. Archard-Thiers syndrome is an unusual combination of virilism and Cushing's.

Ovarian androgen overproduction

The vast majority of hirsuitism occurs because the ovaries have produced too much androgen. This usually results in a group of symptoms called polycystic ovarian syndrome or disease. Externally, this syndrome may be manifested as male pattern hair distribution, or excessive facial, neck, chest and thigh hair, as well as diminutive breasts. Internally, the woman experiences erratic or nonexistent menstrual periods and she may develop cysts on her ovaries. There are also cases of male pattern hair growth where a cause has not been identified, termed idiopathic hirsutism. The adrenal glands can sometimes produce excessive androgens; this is called adrenal hyperplasia. The general term for androgen overproduction is hyperandrogenaemia.

Hirsuitism diagnosis

Hirsutism is caused by overproduction of androgens by either the ovary or the adrenal gland. There are blood tests available that measure the concentrations of sex hormones. Typical hormones quantified are testosterone, free testosterone, androstenedione, DHEA-S, and 17-hydroxyprogesterone. These tests are usually performed several times because hormone levels can vary. More sophisticated scans such as ultrasound are sometimes used as diagnostic tools. The healthcare provider also needs to obtain a thorough history and examination in order to identify the signs and symptoms of the hirsuitism. This is because only some of these signs are external (such as excessive hair growth, oily skin, and acne) and may in fact be absent (such as lack of excessive hair in Oriental females) while internal symptoms may be present (abnormal or absent menstrual periods for example).

Lesser-known enzymes

An enzyme called 5-alpha-reductase catalyzes the reaction that converts testosterone (T) to dihydrotestosterone (DHT) in cells that are sensitive to androgens. This enzyme has been found to be elevated in the skin of hirsute individuals, and its elevation leads to increased urinary levels of androstenediol glucuronide. A deficiency of the enzyme 21-hydroxylase has been found to elevate androgen levels in a small percentage of hirsute women; the mechanism is related to too much formation of 17-hydroxyprogesterone and conversion of cortisol precursors into androgens. Detection of adrenal tumors or carcinomas or presence of Cushing's syndrome suggests hirsutism. Ovarian hormone imbalances are good indications of possible hirsutism as well.

Treatments for hirsutism

Hirsutism can be treated medically by commercially available antiandrogens. One of these antiandrogens is spironolactone (Aldactone); its primary mode of action is the competitive inhibition with testosterone and DHT for androgen receptors. Another agent is cyproterone acetate (Androcur) which is generally found in combination hormone preparations. It acts like a progesterone and is usually combined with an estrogen component; it also has antigonadotropin properties. Another shorter-acting antiandrogen is flutamide (Euflex) which is also a competitive inhibiter for T and DHT. Various hormonal therapies used simultaneously with oral contraceptives or glucocorticoids can control hirsutism as well. Weight loss can diminish expressions of hirsutism by lowering androgen and active testosterone levels.

Hypertrichosis

Sometimes hypertrichosis is generalized, which means that there is excessive body hair in many areas in disproportionate amounts expected for that individual's ethnic group. Many of these cases actually result from taking drugs that suppress the immune system), control seizures, elevate glucose levels, or actually stimulate hair growth. A variety of drugs can also stimulate androgen production and result in hirsuitism. Many cases of hypertrichosis are more localized such as very hairy and heavily pigmented moles and birthmarks. Hair patches can develop when skin areas are being constantly abraded or if hairy skin has been grafted from another part of the body. There is also an uncommon metabolic disorder called porphyria that can result in this phenomenon.

Electrologists are exposed to bodily fluids including blood components. Therefore, knowledge of the principles of microbiology, the study of microorganisms and the consequences of infection with them on other organisms, is essential for the electrologist. There are a number of types of microorganisms, including viruses, fungi, protozoa, fungi, and bacteria. Some bacteria are useful to humans, but others are termed "pathogenic" because they spread disease. Equipment and areas used for electrolysis must be carefully sterilized to prevent dissemination of these microorganisms, and the electrologist needs to wash their hands thoroughly and use personal protective devices to prevent their spread as well.

Bacteria

Bacteria are single-celled microorganisms that have no nucleus or formalized internal structure. They reproduce rapidly, approximately every 20 minutes, utilizing organic material as a food source. They are generally categorized according to their optimal temperature range for growth and their shape. This means that some bacteria will proliferate best in the cold (psychrophiles), while others thrive best at intermediate temperatures (mesophiles) or in very hot environments (thermophiles or the extreme version). Disease-causing bacteria are either round, rodlike, or curved, and they are called cocci, bacilli, or spirilla respectively. Of these, the bacilli, for example tuberculosis, are the most virulent and hardest to destroy because they have projections called cilia that provide motility and they also produce spores. Spores are shielding structures that they bacteria can produce in order to remain dormant when food sources are unavailable. Infections with cocci are characterized by pus formation; a common form is staphylococcus, which is often present in abscesses and pimples. Bacteria can cause localized or systemic infections and can be transmitted by a number of routes.

Fungi, protozoa, and algae

All fungi and some protozoa are parasites; in other words, they survive by feeding off other organisms. Fungi obtain their nutrients from organic materials, ranging from plant sources to human tissue. They reproduce by forming spores which can form extensions called hyphae that attach themselves to the other organic material or organism. Athlete's foot, for example, is a fungal infection. Protozoa are single-celled microorganisms that feed on organic materials; one of the most common human protozoal infections is dysentery which is caused by amoeba. Algae are microorganisms that thrive in aquatic environments; they are not generally associated with human diseases.

Viruses

Viruses are extremely small parasitic particles. They are composed only of genetic material in the form of either deoxyribonucleic acid or ribonucleic acid surrounded by a protein layer. Viruses can only reproduce by invading host cells and utilizing the cellular material of the latter. Until recently, they were very few ways to treat viral infections because viruses are insensitive to antibiotics, but somewhat effective pharmacologic agents are now available that target either the enzyme reverse transcriptase or inhibit proteases. The list of human viral infections is large but the most important viruses for hair removal specialists to be aware of are various hepatitis-causing viruses and human immunodeficiency virus (HIV).

Hepatitis

Hepatitis is a condition in which the liver becomes inflamed and secondary effects such as jaundice occur. Any healthcare or personal service worker who may be exposed to blood or bodily fluids could become infected with hepatitis B (HBV) or hepatitis C (HCV) or to a lesser extent delta hepatitis virus (HDV). There are vaccines available in multi-dose regimens that mitigate the possibility of HBV infection, and they are recommended for electrologists or any healthcare professional because HBV is a very hardy virus. Hepatitis C is less virulent and it often mutates; at present reliable vaccines are generally unavailable. HDV has not been well-studied. Another type of hepatitis-causing virus known as hepatitis A or HAV is spread by contaminated food and water; its effects are generally transient and no enduring liver damage is generally seen.

Acquired immunodeficiency syndrome

AIDS, or acquired immunodeficiency syndrome, is the term for the group of identifying symptoms that occur when infection with a form of HIV or human immunodeficiency virus progresses. These symptoms include inability to fight other infections, propensity for unusual malignancies, and wasting. HIV, HBV, and HCV are all spread by contact with infected serum or bodily fluids as through sexual intercourse or across the placenta from mother to child. Blood transfusions are rarely sources of transmission currently due to very sensitive and specific screening tests. The most likely mode of transmission relevant to the hair removal specialist is through contact with broken skin areas in infected individuals. While the possibility of contracting HIV through this means is small, precautions should nevertheless be taken.

Sanitary precautions

The most important sanitary precautions that electrologists should take are thorough hand washing and use of gloves. Hand washing should be thorough, including lathering with antibacterial liquid pump soap for 10 to 15 seconds, followed by use of disposable not reusable towels. The procedure needs to be repeated any time there is a new customer, when gloves are applied or removed, when there is any possibility of spread of infection through contact with bodily fluids including dispersion through coughing, and every time the professional leaves the room. Gloves should always be worn and changed for each client by electrologists. They can be of various compositions, including neoprene, nitrile, and latex among others, but powder-free vinyl gloves are preferred. Although latex provides the best barrier, many people are allergic to the compound, and powder can be distributed into the environment after gloves are removed. The concentration of microorganisms on impenetrable surfaces can be reduced by the use of disinfectants such as glutaraldehyde. Most disinfectants should not be used on the skin, with the exceptions of 99% isopropyl alcohol or 70% ethyl alcohol.

Sterilization procedures

Sterilization procedures kill all pathogens, including bacteria and their spores as well as viruses. They fall into two categories, either chemical or physical agents. The most commonly used chemical agent is a 2% solution of glutaraldehyde in water, which is used for instruments such as forceps and needles. These instruments are cleaned and then submerged in this solution for at least 10 hours. Equipment can also be sterilized by placing them in an airtight container with the chemical ethylene oxide. Intense heat, either moist or dry, can be used to sterilize equipment. Either an apparatus called an autoclave subjects them to pressurized steam at 250 degrees Fahrenheit for 15 to 20 minutes at 15 pounds per square inch (moist) or they are exposed to even higher temperatures of up to 340°F for 1 to 2 hours in a forced air oven (dry). Boiling instruments for at least 2 minutes is also effective. Irradiation will kill many microbes but it is not very effective against the major threat in electrolysis, Hepatitis B.

<u>Steps</u>

Gloves should always be worn when preparing for and performing sterilization procedures. The first step is to completely wash the equipment to remove artifacts usually in an ultrasonic cleaner if available. The instruments should then be rinsed under a stream of water followed by drying with throwaway paper towels. The technician then puts the equipment into the designated sterilization instrument. Since there are a number types of units that could be utilized for this step, the individual must be familiar with the instructions for its use and must have a chemical or preferably biological indicator in the unit to monitor the sterilization. After the procedure, instruments must be stored in a sterile, covered vessel until use. Any compromise of the container's integrity warrants resterilization, as does a long period before use (typically 24 hours).

<u>Effectiveness</u>

The Center for Disease Control as well as various electrolysis organizations and some states specify ways to monitor the effectiveness of sterilization procedures. The best method is use of kits with biological indicators that are returned to a laboratory to check for evidence of microorganisms. There are some chemical indicators that change color with sterilization as well as tapes that contain chemicals that change color as well, but neither of these identifies true sterilization. There is also a spore test available that checks for evidence of spores or microorganisms.

<u>Equipment</u>

There are certain critical items in the electrolysis office that must be sterilized. These include any equipment that touches blood or bodily fluids including needles and forceps or tweezers. Disposable needles are often utilized on a one time basis and then discarded into either a sharps container (with a biohazard sticker) or an isolyzer needle disposal bottle containing disinfectant. If more permanent needles are used multiple times, then they must be stored temporarily after use in an enzyme solution and then sterilized. Forceps should likewise be put into an enzyme solution after use and sterilized later. The tips that are used on an epilator for each client can be treated and sterilized as above because although they do not actually pierce the skin, they many come in contact with broken skin or membranes. An alternative way of dealing with epilator tips is the use of an ultrasonic cleaner followed by rinsing with water, 1% bleach, and water again. Rollers for anaphoresis and cataphoresis can be similarly treated. Other equipment such as protective eyewear, electrodes, epilator chords, needle holders, and holding containers can merely be washed and disinfected.

Universal Precautions

Universal Precautions are sets of precautions against exposure to blood borne pathogens that have been established by the Center for Disease Control. In addition to thorough washing of hands and use of gloves previously described, there are other guidelines. Anyone who might be exposed to bodily fluids or blood, including electrologists as well as most healthcare workers, are required to follow these procedures. They include wearing personal protective equipment such as laboratory coats, goggles, and masks. The individual must know how to use and if necessary dispose of any sharp or contaminated implements including needles that may be exposed to bodily fluids. If skin is compromised suggesting exposure to pathogens, then it should be thoroughly washed until bleeding stops and then antiseptic and a bandage applied. Any incident should be documented as well as the current and later clients. The procedure can usually be continued if the wound is treated in this manner, but subsequently the exposed individual should be tested at minimum for HIV and HBV.

Alternative Methods of Hair Removal

Folliculitis and pseudofolliculitis barbae

Folliculitis is a situation in which infections develop in the hair follicle leading to inflammation and pustule or raised boil formation in the area. The microorganisms responsible for this condition are either bacteria or fungi. Anyone can get folliculitis, and permanent hair removal in the affected follicle may help alleviate it. Pseudofolliculitis barbae (PFB), on the other hand, is a condition exacerbated by shaving where the follicles become inflamed, irritated, and possibly infected. It usually occurs if the hairs shaved off are very close and sharp, and therefore PFB can usually be prevented by not shaving too closely. PFB also often occurs in black males because their coiled hair can grow back into and infect the skin area.

Shaving

Shaving as a hair removal technique is cheap, quick, relatively painless, and can be done at home. It does not permanently remove hair, and the bristly regrowth occurs within one or several days because androgens in the area are enhanced. In addition, shaving can precipitate cases of PFB and ingrown hairs, it does not distinguish between the terminal hairs the individual wishes to remove and the fine vellus hair in the facial area, and cuts often occur. The last disadvantage makes shaving unsuitable for anyone with diabetes or individuals taking agents that dilute their blood. Shaving can be performed with either an electric or manual razor, preferably with the skin wetted with water or foams. Ideally, the procedure should not be performed in the same area more frequently than every other day. The main considerations are ways to reduce the inflammation that can result with shaving, and these include use of unscented cleansers, addition of tea tree oil to the lubricant, and application after shaving of unscented products that exfoliate (such as alpha hydroxy acid or AHA) and suppress inflammation (like salicylic acid).

Tweezing

Tweezing is a non-permanent method of hair removal that is inexpensive, but it can be very labor intensive, especially in areas with a lot of hair. It is often very difficult to get close enough to really see all the hairs to be removed, and tweezing can often deform the hair. One big advantage of tweezing, however, is that the procedure usually does remove the complete hair, which means that regrowth is not seen as quickly. Repeated tweezing can cause rapid growth of highly pigmented hairs, however. Hair should be pulled out with the tweezers in the direction of preferred regrowth. Numbing solutions containing lidocaine or benzocaine or ice applied to the area before tweezing can alleviate some of the pain involved with the technique. Other lotions are sometimes applied as well, but they can make gripping with the tweezers difficult if they are not removed.

Electronic tweezing and home electrolysis kits

Electronic tweezers are tweezers attached to a source of high-frequency current. In theory they destroy the root of the hair by subjecting the hair shaft to this energy source for up to 30 seconds, but in reality the energy can radiate elsewhere rendering the procedure relatively ineffective as well as potentially dangerous. It should not be used in pregnant females or individuals with pacemakers. Home electrolysis devices are very difficult to self-administer and regulate, and they are contraindicated in a number of diseases. The basic principle of these kits is the conduction of electric current by a salt solution which the individual dips their fingers into. Then the person inserts a wand called a touch band with a pointy end called a stylet into the hair follicle. The root has been reached when the area stings; it can be destroyed by further application for about 15 seconds.

Chemical depilatories

There are a variety of forms of chemical depilatories such as creams and lotions. All of these contain substances that destroy the keratin in the hair. Typical depilatories contain some combination of calcium thioglycolate, sodium thioglycolate and/or sodium hydroxide. The hair breaks off and the chemicals react with it to form gelatinous complexes with the hair that can be easily removed. This procedure really should not be performed more than once every 4 weeks for a variety of reasons. For example, depilation eliminates an excessive amount of dead cells from the skin's surface which means that it takes a long time to replenish this protective skin barrier. The skin can therefore become irritated. While use of chemical depilatories is easy and not too expensive and does result in softer hair re-growth, the possibility of irritation or infection is a big disadvantage of this technique. A facial depilatory should be less strong than one employed in other areas.

Bleaches, abrasives, and mechanical epilation devices

Hair growth can be disguised with the topical use of bleaching agents that remove the pigment of the hair but not the hair itself. Hydrogen peroxide is an oxidating agent. It is activated by ammonium bicarbonate, and oxidation and bleaching results. This procedure cannot be done near any sensitive areas like the eyes or in any places that are irritated or have open cuts. There are a variety of abrasive tools like pumice stones that rub off surface hair (as well as dead skin), but again these devices can cause irritation and pain, rapid hair re-growth, and follicle deformation. There are also electric coils available that perform what is termed mechanical epilation. These devices are primarily utilized on the leg hairs, and they work by rotating and pulling out several hairs at a time. This is a relatively painful procedure, but it may result in slow and soft further growth.

Hair reduction creams

Hair reduction creams are topical treatments that slow down re-growth of hair. They are usually used in conjunction with other techniques. The most useful products require a prescription, and the chemical eflornithine is the most widespread substance included. Eflornithine acts by inhibiting metabolic processes in the hair follicle itself by blocking the enzymatic catalyst ornithine decarboxylase. These creams can cause folliculitis and other transient irritations, but have been found to relatively safe. The downside, however, is that they sort of defeat the purpose of the actual hair removal technique by extending the time between treatments.

Home waxing kits

The advantages of home waxing kits are convenience, low cost, and confidentiality (particularly when waxing certain private areas). The types and operating temperatures of kits available are numerous, but all are pretty messy and hard to thermoregulate. There is a learning curve involved with learning to wax in the correct direction, to avoid breakage of the hair, and to prevent burning, bruising, or adherence of the wax to the skin. Some of the most common areas that are waxed such as the eyebrows or bikini areas are not only difficult to self-wax but errors can be hazardous as well.

Threading

Threading is a hair removal technique utilized for hundreds of years in Middle Eastern countries that uses a sterile thread to pull out hairs in the facial area. Sterilization of the cotton thread is performed in an ultraviolet sterilizer in modern times. The portion of the skin to be threaded needs to be separated from other hair, devoid of makeup, cleaned with an antiseptic, and permitted to dry before beginning the procedure. The threads are typically 2 to 2 ½ feet long and the ends are tied together. The loop is then manipulated and twisted with the fingers of the technician to pluck out hairs at a rapid pace. Lotions may be administered afterwards. The technique is relatively inexpensive and less painful than many other processes. However, threading does distort the hair follicle, and it can predispose the individual to other problems such as folliculitis upon re-growth. Threading is inappropriate for larger, irritated, damaged, or sunburned skin areas. It should not be performed on anyone with skin diseases like psoriasis.

Sugaring method

Sugaring is an ancient technique of hair removal developed and still often practiced in Middle Eastern and Mediterranean areas. Originally, it was discovered that a sugar paste applied to wounds also removed hair when pulled off without annoying the area at the same time. Afterwards only a warm, slightly wet cloth was applied. The procedure was and can still be an inexpensive home technique. However, there are now kits available that modify this ancient methodology and make it somewhat more irritating to the skin and hair follicle. This is because there are either additional ingredients like sticky resins added or the mixture is removed with a muslin strip. The basic formula for a sugar paste is an 8:1:1 ratio of sugar to lemon juice and water, which is slowly heated and then cooled off.

Current types

Today there are two different methods of sugaring for hair removal; they are distinguished by the methods of application and removal. Each requires cleaning the skin area with an antibacterial agent followed by unscented non-irritating powder to soak up moisture. The technician should wear gloves. In the first technique, the sugar paste is formed into a ball and then manually applied by hand in the direction opposing hair growth and then pulled off in the same path as growth. This is repeated usually with the same mass of paste until removal is complete. Since the hair shaft and even part of the follicle is saturated, breakage and follicle deformation should be minimized. An alternative method uses a spatula to apply the paste in the same track as hair growth, and then a muslin strip is applied and subsequently pulled off in the direction opposite the hair growth. The latter method is similar in many ways to hot waxing.

Advantages and disadvantages

The hand application method of sugaring is more universally applicable. The list of diseases and disorders that preclude the spatula application and strip removal technique is extensive, ranging from skin disorders and varicose veins to diabetes, circulation problems and epilepsy. The hand method should still be avoided if skin is irregular or damaged in any way, during pregnancy or episodes of herpes simplex sores, and approval of the client's doctor is required for a few primarily circulatory disorders. Nevertheless, the advantages of the hand application method far outweigh the disadvantages. This technique causes minimal irritation and bruising, does not distort the follicle or break hairs, and is very hygienic because the paste is an inherent bacteriostat. If the spatula application method is used at cooler temperatures without addition of resins, the disadvantages are minimized, but there is still a greater chance of development of folliculitis, ingrown hairs, and irritation with this technique.

Waxing

Pre-waxing protocol

Prior to waxing, especially for a new client, the individual should be questioned about existing conditions and informed about preparation for the procedure. It is usually preferable to have a signed release form from the client and another card that chronicles some of the client's specific issues. The client should be informed either on the phone or at the salon about some of the prerequisites and possible side effects of the technique. Specifically, they should know that the hair needs to be at least a quarter to half inch long depending on whether it is fine or coarse, ingrown hairs should be corrected and permitted to heal for several days prior to the procedure, the area should be exfoliated prior to but not on the day of the waxing, and tanning immediately prior to or after the removal is unacceptable. They should be made aware that the procedure might cause transient redness, puffiness, or surface dots of blood.

Waxes

Waxes are solid compounds that can be dissolved in organic liquids such as benzene but not in aqueous solutions such as water or alcohol. They can be derived from many natural forms as well as synthesized in the laboratory. Waxes may or may not have crystalline structures, and their consistencies vary greatly, but all can be melted to a compliant state. The type of wax that is predominantly utilized for hair removal is called honey wax which has a sticky tree resin called gum rosin added to it. This honey wax is most often applied hot and then pulled off with a strip, but it can be an irritant so skin calming agents such as azulene from chamomile are often added. The other major type of wax used is hard beeswax. The latter is especially useful in areas that are delicate or that have erratic hair directions.

<u>Advantages and disadvantages</u>

The main advantages of waxing for hair removal are that the technique is expeditious and that it eradicates the hair deeply into the shaft often into the root. The latter means that the

- 29 -

period of time until re-growth is evident is long, up to 2 months, and growth can even be reduced. On the negative side, however, skin irritation can result from too hot wax or the resins in the wax, there is a high incidence of hair breakage, and subsequent growth can be erratic because the hair has been distorted or pulled off in various directions. The hair has to be fairly long to perform this technique, about a half inch for coarser hair. This method cannot be used on clients taking any drug that makes the skin delicate and dehydrated such as Retin-A or other acne medications, with anyone taking any drug including birth control pills that contain tetracycline, or people taking blood thinners or other agents that predispose them to bruising. There is also an extensive list of disorders, similar to that for sugaring, which precludes use of waxing for hair removal.

Ingrown hairs

Typically, ingrown hairs are usually observed as either blackheads or thin lines of ingrown hair. Sometimes the client can release these ingrown hairs themselves with a sterile sharp tweezers, but this must be done at least 4 days before their appointment so that the follicle can mend. Instead, release of the ingrown hairs is often performed at the salon by the technician. If the form is a blackhead, the hair removal specialist can generally extract the hair prior to the waxing by cleansing the area with alcohol and lightly constricting the blackhead. If the ingrown hair is observed as a thin line, then release should be done after the procedure. In this case, the area is wiped with alcohol and the hair released with a sterile pointed tweezers, but the actually hair should not be pulled out for several days to allow for follicle normalization. If venipuncture type needles are used to release the hair, they should be recapped and disposed of in the sharps container. Gloves should always be worn for both types of extraction.

Preparing waxing client

The setup of the treatment room must be ergonomic or designed for ease of use. It must be well lighted and a magnifying lamp should be available. If more private areas such as the bikini line are to be waxed, an isolated room should be used. A variety of agents to cleanse the client's skin prior to waxing are required. The technician may need to remove the individual's makeup in certain areas. The skin area should be cleansed with the agents provided in the kit. Except for the facial area, an included numbing reagent is then applied. Pure tea tree oil is generally sparingly spread over the region as a bacteriostatic and calming agent. Dusting powder is sprinkled on the skin and hair. After the waxing, undesired situations are addressed. These include removal of stubborn lingering wax with lotions, reduction of swelling with application of cold packs or ice, or soothing of hives. Hives are actually allergic reactions that may be calmed with provided reagents or cool compresses or preferably an antihistamine such as Benadryl.

Double dipping

Double dipping is a practice disallowed by a few state cosmetology organizations in which the technician re-dips and reuses the same applicator for spreading wax. Double dipping probably does not promote growth of bacteria because most bacteria will die above 140°F which is generally below the temperature of the heated wax pot; in addition, no water is present in the wax to promote reproduction. Viruses such as HBV may not be killed until the pasteurization temperature of 159°F is achieved, but government organizations have shown no concern about the possibility of viral contamination. In fact, risk is minimized because only the wax but not the applicator touches the client.

Safety procedures

The waxing unit should never contact water, not only because it is an electrical device, but also because wax only dissolves in organic solvents and water promotes proliferation of bacteria. The heating unit should be unplugged when not in use and never left unattended. The heater must be connected to and grounded into certified outlets only in order to avoid shocking in the event of a short circuit. Cords and aeration openings for the unit must be unobstructed and free of other heat sources. The unit should only be repaired by the manufacturer or its authorized representative.

Depilatory wax technique

Hard depilatory wax is generally a combination of vegetable waxes obtained from the candelilla plant and the carnauba palm tree, beeswax, and a resin called rosin coming from components of pine trees. This is because the goal is to maintain the temperature near or somewhat above that of the body; this enables the wax to harden after application as it cools down. Since it is difficult to find one wax that melts at the preferred temperature range for application, approximately 125 to 140°F, a mixture is needed. The wax mixture can be heated up to about 165°F maximum because it does cool quickly.

Advantages

Hard wax combinations are heated to lower melting points and they are inherently thicker than waxes used in the strip method. This means that the hard waxes cool down and set quickly. At first they are applied against the route of hair growth, which allows the wax to saturate the base of the hair shaft and tightly grasp the hair. Subsequently, other layers of wax are added. The wax is then usually removed in the direction of the hair growth, preventing distortion of the follicle. The wax itself does not stick to the skin, making this technique less irritating than strip waxing and suitable for use more sensitive areas. The latter observation means that hard depilatory wax can often be used for clients where other techniques are contraindicated, such as those who are using acne medications or skincare products containing alpha hydroxy or glycolic acids. There is a longer period before re-growth is observed as well, generally 1 ½ to 3 months.

Negative aspects

Using the non-strip hard depilatory wax method of hair removal is tedious and labor intensive, rendering it generally unsuitable for use on larger body areas. New wax must be added every day and blended well, and it is crucial not to heat the wax either too much or continuously because it can solidify and become brittle and dark. If the patron is retaining water such as during menstruation, it is difficult to use this technique because the hairs shrivel into the tightened skin. The contraindications for use of the hard wax technique are similar to many other hair removal techniques, ranging from various types of lesions and skin disorders or product use to a number of circulatory disorders and severe cases of diabetes.

Eyebrow wax procedure

During the eyebrow wax procedure, the client should be prone or in a partially reclined position. Makeup should be taken off and the eyebrow region cleansed with a gentle antiseptic solution. Tea tree oil should be applied followed by a dusting powder. The temperature of the wax needs to be checked on the technician's wrist during this time. Then wax is spread under the brow, initially against the direction of hair growth and then parallel to it. This is continued until both hairs and skin are completely covered, and the wax should remain until its glossy, tacky consistency changes to a more opaque appearance. The wax is removed in this case against the direction of hair growth by holding the skin tightly with one thumb and pulling it off from the outer edge inward. Sometimes wax is also similarly applied to and removed from the region between the eyebrows, called the glabellar area. Removal should be followed by application of antiseptic lotion and a soft massaging of the area culminating in the temple region.

Upper lip area

Client positioning and technician preparation for hard waxing the upper lip area both resemble the procedures for waxing the eyebrows. When actually applying the hard wax to the upper lip, the technician should stand in back of the client near their head. The wax is initially applied against the hair growth, meaning from the outer corner to the center, and then reversed, and the process is repeated until the wax layer is about an eighth of an inch thick. For fine hair, removal can be done in the same path as hair growth, which is downward; this is preferable if possible because the skin in the upper lip area is more fragile than other parts like the eyebrow area. However, thicker hairs may not come out unless removed against the direction of hair growth. After hair removal, the technician should press their index finger against the upper lip to alleviate the stinging usually experienced by the client, and then they should apply an antiseptic lotion.

Non-strip waxing

<u>Chin area</u>

Preparation and post-treatment for non-strip hot waxing of the chin area is similar to that used for other areas. Both the chin and sides of the face have a significant relative amount of fine vellus hair relative to the amount of coarser terminal hair, however. Therefore, the direction of removal should be determined with this mind, with predominantly vellus hair removal in the direction of hair growth to prevent follicle distortion, and extrusion of regions of terminal or erratic growth against the hair growth. In the case of the chin, the technician should position themselves in back of the client, and spread the wax in 2-inch by 3-inch sections against and then with the hair growth. The bottom of the chin should be done before the actual chin area, which needs to be waxed in very small sections.

<u>Sides of the face</u>

Standard preparatory and after-treatment procedures are followed for hot waxing of the sides of the face. This area has a relatively large proportion of fine vellus hair just like the chin, which means removal is in the direction of hair growth. For the sides of the face, scalp hair must be kept away from the area by some means, and any hair longer than a half inch needs to be pre-trimmed to that length. One side of the face is waxed at a time so the client's head needs to be tilted. Application of wax against and then with the growth direction needs to be done until a layer about one eighth inch is spread.

Hard waxing

<u>Underarm area</u>

In order for the technician to wax the underarm area, the client must take off clothes covering the area and lie prone on a provided table with a modesty drape. Blots of blood usually develop so use of gloves is mandatory. The skin is thoroughly cleaned and then dried with dusting powder to get rid of sweat and deodorant. Longer hairs may need to be trimmed to about one half inch before waxing. The client lifts the arm to be waxed and positions the inner surface of that hand under their head while shielding the breast with their other hand. Small sections, about 1 by 2 inches, should be waxed starting at the outer portion of the underarm and working inward. The direction of hair growth may be erratic under the arms. Wax is spread on first against and then with the perceived path of growth and removed against it. After waxing, antiseptic lotions and possibly cooled cotton bandages soaked in water and baking soda may need to be placed over the area to assuage possible irritation. Contraindications include mastitis or previous breast removal.

<u>Forearms</u>

It is very time consuming to hard wax the forearms, and strip waxing is often done instead. If hair has not been previously removed from this area and the growth is still relatively fine and orderly, then hard waxing is a good choice. The client is seated and wears protective clothing, and the technician is facing them. After cleansing and powdering the forearms, initially the inside of the forearm is waxed with the individual extending their arms with the palms up and waxing long 2 inch wide patches up the arm. Hair growth on the arms runs down toward the wrist so the sequence of waxing is away from the wrist and growth followed by downward parallel to growth, and then the wax is removed in the direction of growth. With palms facing downward, the technician then does similar patching and removal on the outside of the arm. The last section can be done by having the client lift their arm and waxing in one or two large pieces between the elbow and the little finger; here the hair growth runs toward the elbow so the wax is the application and removal is the opposite of the other parts of the arm. The irritation from removal can be alleviated with pressure, and later a salve should be applied.

Hands

The hands and fingers have complex hair growth patterns. The hand should be waxed first, with the client clenching their fist to tighten the skin. One large patch of wax should be applied in the opposite direction to hair growth, then parallel to it, and then the wax is removed in the direction of hair growth. Here the pattern of development of hair is usually from wrist to fingers with a slight slant toward the little finger. Then each finger is waxed in sequence beginning with the thumb and removed after all are set in a similar manner. On the fingers, the pattern of hair growth is generally from either end of the digit to the middle knuckle, and the waxing pattern is against followed by with the hair growth and then removal with the hair growth if possible. Afterwards a calming salve should be kneaded into the area.

Bikini area

Bikini area waxing procedures fall into several classifications based on the extent of the area to be waxed and amount of hair removed. A standard, or American, bikini wax removes the least amount of hair, generally just the hair that would be exposed when wearing a bikini; this usually means right below the navel on the abdomen and up to the panty line on the thigh. The French variety of bikini wax eliminates more hair in the pubic area extending to the anus and labia, resulting in just a narrow frontal band of hair. The Brazilian form of the bikini waxing removes everything in the area. All of these procedures require provisions for the privacy of the client, and at the time of booking they should be made fully aware of the requirements of each in order to choose the right technique that they are comfortable with.

American or standard bikini wax

A standard or American type of bikini wax is usually done by the strip waxing method, but can be performed utilizing hard wax. The client's bathing suit or underwear edges need to be covered with paper towels as shields. The hair is drawn out from under the garment with a tool for visibility; lengthy hairs should be trimmed to about a half inch. The usual pre-wax procedures are performed. The client is prone with one leg on the side held out straight and the other one bent. The customer aids the technician by placing one hand on the paper and one against the bent thigh. Hair growth is downward along the panty line. All hairs are the coarser terminal type which means removal against the direction of growth. Application and removal is performed on the bent leg, beginning in the top region of the inner thigh up to what is called the femoral ridge, and then working downward into the pubic area by slightly lifting the bent leg. Application patches are 2 inches wide, about twice as long, and the sequence is up against the grain, downward with the growth, removal against the growth pattern in one quick and complete action, and application of pressure.

Hot wax strip method

Strip waxing is usually preferred for this type of bikini wax. The hot strip wax used is either a regular honey-containing preparation or wax to which creams have been added. The client is prone, keeps one leg straight, and bends the other while assisting the technician by holding the underwear or swimsuit area away from the waxing. Starting at the bikini line at the front, wax is spread in the direction of the hair proliferation downward along the ridge until the pubis bone is reached. Here growth is directed more toward the center. Strips are placed and rubbed down, and removed quickly and thoroughly against the hair growth. The hair behind the femoral ridge can then be extracted in two sections by lifting the leg more, spreading wax downward along the continued bikini line, similarly applying strips, and then pulling them off upwards against the hair growth. Upper leg hairs can be easily removed from this position as well.

French bikini wax

Hard waxing is the preferred method for removing the additional hair covered by a French bikini wax. Gloves must be worn by the technician and disposable panties by the customer for these procedures. After the standard portion of a bikini wax is performed, in a French version the hair between the buttocks is then hard waxed by having the client either (1) having them raise their knees all the way to their chest with the bottoms of the feet together, or (2) kneeling. The customer can aid in removal with their hand, and the application in either case is against hair growth (up if lying down, down if kneeling) followed by parallel to it, and removal is against the direction of growth. This procedure is followed by excision of hairs in the labia region by saturation of the area with repeated small applications of wax and then removal in the general direction of growth (usually inward or possibly upward) and subsequent application of pressure.

Brazilian bikini wax

In the Brazilian version of the bikini wax, everything performed in the French wax is done, plus hard waxing is also performed on the actual pubis. Blood spotting is very likely to occur, and the customer should be informed of this. The procedures for either a French or Brazilian bikini wax take longer than many other hot waxing techniques, typically up to three-quarters of an hour, and generally can be expected to last up to 6 weeks. Post-removal procedures include applying salve and possibly salicylic acid.

Abdominal region, feet, toes, and legs

The abdominal region is routinely waxed as part of a bikini wax. While the client is prone and panties protected with toweling, the hair is waxed in small sections starting near the navel and moving outward along the panty line. The hair growth pattern in this area is toward the navel, and the wax is usually removed by pulling away from the growth and navel while holding the skin tightly. If feet are waxed, growth is downward toward the toes, and removal is generally against the pattern or toward the leg. Toe hair, which is usually strong and coarse, should be removed against the pattern also, which must be determined by observation; all toes going from the little to the big toe are waxed before pulling the wax off. Hard waxing of the legs is not usually performed because it is too labor intensive, and strip waxing is preferred.

The bikini line of the abdominal area is similarly treated by hot and strip waxing methods in that application is in small sections in the direction of hair growth, starting from the central navel region, and removal is against the path of hair development. If the customer experiences the relatively common situation in which some darker hairs are present in the navel region, other procedures to eliminate these hairs may be warranted. These alternatives to waxing include laser removal, electrolysis, or selective individual excision with spots of wax. If the individual chooses to have the entire region waxed, they must be informed that re-growth will probably be erratic and more pronounced.

Male clients

<u>Eyebrows</u>

Sometimes men have their eyebrows waxed. They may have longer erratically growing hairs that need to cut down before the procedure. The area under the brow is waxed as indicated for any client but care should be taken not to wax the area too extensively to avoid giving the brow a feminine appearance. In addition, men often have hair in the central glabellar region between the brows that can be removed until the part above the inner corner of the eye is reached. The outside edge and lobes of the ear are sometimes waxed in men as well, often by the hot wax strip method. In both of these procedures, the man is usually prone or partially reclined. Removal is against the hair growth pattern, which means pulling upward on the earlobe while grasping it with the other hand.

Chest region

Before waxing the male customer's chest area, the technician should inquire about the extent of the waxing desired; only shoulder area removal may be sufficient. The customer is prone, and the technician is situated on the side to be waxed. Usually hairs need to be pretrimmed to about a half inch long. The entire section to be waxed is then sprayed with an antiseptic like witch hazel, patted dry, and dusted. Wax is spread against the direction of hair growth in relatively large sections starting at the peripheral sparser areas and moving up the chest and in toward the center. In the latter denser areas, sections should be smaller. After application, strips are adhered in the same direction and then pulled off in the opposite path against the hair growth. Pressure is employed each time. The technician then moves to the other side to continue, and at the end calming antiseptic lotions are applied. This is a long procedure, taking as long as three quarters of an hour.

Back

Typically, male customers requesting hair removal from the back want all hairs above their waist excised. The trouser area must be blocked off with toweling. The client lies downward on a table with their head tilted to the side resting on their hands. The technician must don gloves because blood spots are common. Hairs longer than a half inch need to be trimmed first. The area is sprayed with antiseptic and then toweled dry and dusted. Hair growth on the back is from the outer edges inward, so the technician stands on one side and applies the wax in large sections from the periphery to the center beginning at the waist and proceeding upwards. Strips are applied in the direction of growth and removed by pulling in the opposing direction. If using a single strip in one section is difficult, multiple strips starting at the outside are sometimes utilized. At the very top in the middle, hairs grow downward; therefore, that is the direction of application there. After the other side is waxed, the client may sit up and have their shoulders waxed. In addition to the usual antiseptic lotion, cooling bandages saturated with baking powder may be necessary because temporary hives often occur.

Hot wax strip method

The hot wax strip method of hair removal is now performed in many areas of the body, but it is especially preferred for extracting hair from larger regions like the back because the technique is less labor intensive than hard waxing. Some of these hard "waxes" actually contain wax, typically beeswax, along with the pine resins called rosins. Others simply contain honey combined with a refined version of the rosin called glycerol ester. Many add calming agents such as tea tree oil. Application in smaller areas such as the eyebrow is usually done with disposable wooden spatulas, but other means of application are available for larger areas, including special applicators or rollers provided with the waxing kit.

Basic principles

The hot wax strip method of hair removal is conducted by applying a heated and relatively runny wax solution in the direction of hair growth, and then adhering and pulling off a strip against the direction of hair proliferation. Since most of these preparations are kits including the heating apparatus, provided instructions should be followed. In general, however, the temperature and consistency of the "wax" should be tested (usually on the technician's arm), the preparation should be applied in sections at a 45 degree angle to the skin, a strip should be placed over the area and patted down briefly for adherence, and then the strip should be rapidly removed while applying pressure to the adjacent skin. Strips are usually made out of either untreated muslin or pellon, and they can be reused on the same client because the wax accumulation actually enhances removal. Afterwards, some sort of antiseptic is usually applied.

Advantages and disadvantages

The hot wax strip method of hair removal is generally contraindicated for any of the conditions that preclude any hot wax method including a variety of circulatory and infectious disorders, presence of an array of skin lesions or disorders, varicose veins, use of topical anti-acne preparations, and use of drugs containing tetracycline. The hot wax strip technique does have some advantages centering on its speed of use and subsequent negligible irritation. In addition, this method opens up the pores and saturates the hair shaft all the way down to in some cases the follicle root; this means re-growth is generally softer and occurs later. On the other hand, one of the primary disadvantages of the strip method is that hair is removed against the direction of growth precluding its use in sensitive (Brazilian bikini) or erratic (underarm) growth areas, and thus it also results in multidirectional re-growth. When additional strip waxes are performed in the same area, it is difficult often to identify the growth pattern. The rosins in the wax can irritate the skin as well.

Forehead

If a woman has some sort of irregular hairline including what is known as a widow's peak, she may want that area of the forehead balanced out with hair removal. Usually electrolysis or a gentle waxing procedure are the methods of choice but sometimes strip waxing is performed. If the latter technique is used, the identified removal area should be segregated from other scalp hair and trimmed to about a quarter inch long. After standard cleaning and powdering procedures, small areas of wax are spread in the path of hair growth and muslin strips applied the same way and gently massaged in place. These strips should be longer than the portion covered so that the end can be secured with one hand and rapidly pulled off while the skin is kept tight with the technician's other hand. Pressure is applied briefly, and lotion put on the area after all desired hairs are removed in a similar fashion.

Eyebrows

After determining the correct shaping for the female client's eyebrow area, the region is cleaned, makeup is taken off, tea tree oil is rubbed in, and the area is dusted in preparation. The underneath portion of the brow itself is waxed first by smearing small amounts in direction of growth along this area while pulling the skin away from the brow. A strip is put over the waxed area and massaged rapidly in the same direction, and then the strip is quickly pulled off in the opposite direction using the free end while the skin is kept taut with other fingers. After both eyebrows are waxed, the central glabellar region can be done; application is upward while removal is downward. Lastly, some hairs may still need tweezing, and then calming salves are applied to the area. For men, the technique is similar but arching is not crucial and a more natural look is desired.

A good technician learns to shape the eyebrow in a manner flattering and appropriate to the age and lifestyle of the client. Generally, older and more professional women prefer thinner and more arched eyebrows than the younger client. The shape of the individual's face is important, because skilled arching can affect how it is perceived. In general, the top of the arch should be closer to the center for people with wide-set eyes or a round face (generally right above the pupil) and further outside the pupil for individuals with a narrow face or close-set eyes. The inside edge of the brow should start just above the outside edge of the nostril (determined by holding a stick upright and parallel to the edge), the point of the arch should be determined using the same stick and applying the above rules, and the brow should end at the point where the brow naturally meets a line drawn from the base of the nose through the outside edge of the eye.

Upper lip area

The upper lip area is very sensitive and creams are usually added to the waxes used for strip removal in this area. Standard preparation procedures are performed, and then one side of the upper lip is waxed beginning in the central area under the septum of the nose and moving outward along the lip line. In general, this is the direction of hair growth although hairs develop straight downward directly under the nose. An inch thick strip is put on top and then quickly removed against the hair growth by holding the outer edge and pulling it off toward the center. The technician then briefly applies pressure to reduce the pain and proceeds to the other lip. At the end, it helps to softly rub the area, and sometimes ice is applied if there is pain or swelling.

Sides of the face

The sides of the face are supposed to have hair on them, and it is primarily vellus hair. Removal is usually not really recommended but if done electrolysis is preferred to reduce follicle distortion and magnified, distorted re-growth. Menopause can trigger androgen overproduction and depression of estrogen in women, and this is the time some terminal hair may be observed. Hard waxing (or possibly sugaring) is again preferable to strip waxing in this area. If strip waxing is selected, scalp hair should be segregated away from the face and any long portions of hair to be removed should be trimmed to about one half inch long. After usual preparations of the area, the head is tilted to the side. Wax is spread over the desired areas parallel to the growth path (down and toward the center), a strip is added, and then the strip is pulled off against the direction of hair growth. If multiple strips are needed, removal usually begins closest to the nose. After the other side is similarly treated, calming lotions are applied.

<u>Female underarm region</u>

Hair growth is erratic in the underarm region. Hard waxing is a better procedure for this area than strip waxing because it fully saturates the hair follicle and then contracts and hoists the hair away from the skin. If strip waxing is done, then preparatory procedures are similar to that used when hard waxing the area. The technician should always wear gloves because blood nodules can form. While prone, the client raises the arm to be waxed and puts that hand behind their head, opening up the area for removal. The professional is situated behind the client's head. Wax is spread on parallel to the path of hair growth holding the applicator at a 45 degree angle. A strip is applied and secured and then the wax is pulled off against the path of hair proliferation. This is followed by the usual pressure. After the entire area has been waxed, lotion and possibly cool compresses containing baking soda solutions are put on the underarm. Then the other arm is waxed similarly.

<u>Woman's arm and hand regions</u>

If these areas are strip waxed, the biggest difference is that wax should be applied in the direction of the hair growth before a strip is applied and then pulled off against the path of the hair. In other words, for the forearms, the technician faces the seated client and applies the wax in downward sections starting at the wrist on the inner arm, in strokes going from the inner to outer edges on the top, and along the outer rim from the wrist to the elbow. The same strips can be used to grab unsightly hairs in the upper arm region if present. Removal procedures for the hand are similar to the hard wax methods described, except wax is again applied parallel to hair growth, a strip added, and then the strip and hair are pulled out against the direction of growth.

Chin waxing

Generally, electrolysis is the preferred method for hair removal in the chin and jaw areas because waxing promotes further and more visible, pronounced hair re-growth. This is because the area has no innate border lines such as the lip or eyebrow. It is impossible to remove only terminal and not adjacent vellus hairs. Hard waxing is easier to control than strip waxing. If the latter technique is selected, then the area is prepared and the reclining client holds their head back. The technician spreads wax in the direction of hair growth starting at the jawbone and moving toward the neck. Growth at the base of the neck is more outward from the center. To remove that hair, several strips may need to be applied and then removed against the hair growth while manually holding the skin taut at the throat area. If desired, the jaw area is then waxed by applying several small patches of wax that do not intersect planes of the jaw. Alternatively, small dots of wax may be put on individual terminal hairs and removed singly by pressure and pulling.

Strip waxing of the lower legs

For strip wax removal of lower leg hair, the client is prone and antiseptic spray and dusting powder is applied extensively including the back of the legs while bent. Excess moisture is removed with tissues. If feet are to be waxed too, they are done first by application with and removal against the path of growth. The inside portion of the lower leg is then waxed in approximately seven inch sections descending parallel to the path of growth starting near the ankle and moving up the leg to the knee. Strips are applied, massaged in, and pulled off upwards away from the path of growth. The leg is swiveled outward and sections going up the inside of the leg starting near the shin are waxed and then rotated inward to remove hair on the outside of the lower leg. Knees can be waxed in the bent position by spreading wax downward and removing strips by pulling up. The customer turns over and dangles their feet off the edge of the table for removal of hair from the back of the legs. Waxing of the rear calf area is done in sections from the outer edge to the inside in the direction of growth there. Behind the knee, the path of hair growth needs can be erratic.

Upper leg wax

When a full leg wax encompassing the upper areas of the leg is to be done, front waxing continues on the same leg up the thigh. First, the middle section is waxed in portions with

- 44 -

application downwards parallel to hair growth, and removal in the opposite direction. Hair on either side of this central portion generally grows in a descending but slightly outward arcing path and on the back of the thigh it ascends, so that should be kept in mind for subsequent removal procedures. The inner and outer thighs can be reached with rotation, and the back can be done with the knee bent. In order to reach the area near the buttocks, the client needs to lift their knee all the way to their chest. Any removal in the thigh region should be done while holding the relatively loose skin tautly. Regardless of whether the leg waxing is complete or only in the lower leg, this is a stressful procedure and tender stroking of the entire area with the hands (effleurage) is recommended.

Permanent Hair Removal

Electrology

Electrology is a general term for the investigation of electricity and its traits. Electrolysis, on the other hand, is the application of electrical current to destroy materials, and as applied to hair removal, the term really means employment of this current to aid in the removal of hair or skin surface lesions. The hair removal is permanent because the root is destroyed by the electric current. The most effective electrolysis technique is called galvanic electrolysis, which employs a direct current. Another method is known as thermolysis, which utilizes a high frequency current; this technique is faster but may not destroy certain follicles. There is also a blend method which combines elements of both.

Electrolysis

Ophthalmologist Dr. Charles E. Michel started in 1869 and documented in 1875 studies that showed that ingrown eyelashes could be permanently removed by placing a surgical needle attached to a dry cell in the hair follicle. This application of direct current was further refined by a Paul Kree, a New York professor; he expanded the technique to simultaneous use of 6 needles. This method, galvanic electrolysis, is now widespread, and its basic mode of action is destruction by caustic lye that is generated. Another type of electrolysis employing higher frequency currents was described by Dr. Henri Bordier from Lyon, France in 1924. The technique elucidated by Dr. Bordier breaks down substances by the heat generated and has been termed thermolysis or diathermy (meaning to heat). A machine that blends the use of the two techniques was patented by Henri St. Pierre and Arthur Hinkel in 1948, although the work was begun a decade earlier. The speed of the "blend" method is somewhere between galvanic electrolysis and thermolysis; it is the technique most often used for permanent hair removal in the United States.

Client consultation

A client consultation prior to beginning the actual electrolysis procedure is paramount. The initial phone contact should ideally be between the client and the technician, who can explain what is involved. If this task is left to administrative personnel, they should receive some basic education about the procedure and professional staff. At the onsite consultation, the technician examines the area and explains their recommendations and procedures before any work is actually done. This is supplemented by a questionnaire that addresses medical history, medications, and prior use of hair removal procedures. The client also needs to be informed about re-growth, inter-treatment home care and temporary removal guidelines, and potential side effects.

Health history

Before beginning electrolysis, the hair removal specialist should obtain the client's health history and if possible medications being taken. A number of skin disorders may preclude treatment temporarily or in some cases permanently. Sunburned or inflamed skin areas should not undergo electrolysis until these conditions have subsided. Teenagers and adults with acne vulgaris should not undergo electrolysis during an active outbreak because the procedure can spread the bacteria associated with acne and it compounds the associated pain. Individuals undergoing active episodes of herpes virus cold sore should temporarily forego electrolysis as well, although sometimes this can be controlled by taking antiviral medications prior to the visit. If the client has eczema on their skin, the affected area cannot be subjected to electrolysis, but clear skin regions can be done. Electrolysis should not be done on moles unless they have first been medically examined to exclude the presence of cancerous cells.

Medical conditions

One of the most important medical conditions requiring physician approval before electrolysis is diabetes. Diabetics have diminished responses to touch and pain in the lower extremities, which means electrolysis in those regions is contraindicated. In addition, these individuals do not heal well so extraordinary sanitary precautions are necessary. The current generated during electrolysis can exacerbate attacks in epileptics. People with various heart conditions should be treated in short bouts and carefully as well because they may have circulatory problems, tendencies toward bruising, high blood pressure, and more. Galvanic or blend type procedures are usually contraindicated for individuals with implanted pacemakers; guidelines to avoid interference with the pacemaker must be strictly adhered to if they are performed. Individuals with conditions that can be aggravated by use of electrolysis, like asthma and high blood pressure, must be closely monitored. The direct current used with galvanic treatments can cause pain in any areas with metal implants, so thermolysis is the preferred method in those regions.

Local anesthesia

Since there is often pain associated with electrolysis, local anesthesia is frequently used to numb the discomfort. The available products include both prescription and non-prescription preparations. The most widely used topical product available by prescription is called eutectic mixture of local anesthetics (EMLA) and it contains prilocaine and lidocaine. These drugs vasoconstrict or narrow blood vessels and therefore lower the rate of blood flow. EMLA is applied well before the actual electrolysis, about ¾ of an hour prior to it, and the area is wrapped with an occlusive dressing until the electrolysis is begun. Then the preparation is massaged into the area; this should numb the section for about a half hour. There are also non-prescription topical preparations available as well, generally containing lidocaine or another anesthetic called benzocaine. Essentially the best application process for these is similar to the EMLA and requires an occlusive dressing. Alternatively, they are often applied to sections adjacent to the part undergoing electrolysis for short periods of just a few minutes as the technician proceeds.

Preparation of the treatment area

The treatment area should be wiped with a mild cleanser. This is usually followed by swabbing with antiseptic alcohol preparations, usually 70% ethanol or sometimes isopropyl alcohol, to kill microorganisms. Gentler preparations like witch hazel are used in more vulnerable regions. A topical numbing cream is usually then put on the area (unless it has been previously applied). The needle holder is swabbed with an alcohol preparation and a sterile probe attached at that time. The positive electrode is readied by either adding conducting gel or saturating a pad, which is given to the customer to grasp. Some method of collecting the removed hair needs to be set up as well. The electrolysis machine is set to the selected readings.

Relaxing patient

One of the most important things to do before beginning electrolysis is to drape off the area to be treated, especially if it is sensitive. The idea is also to inspire confidence from the client by washing hands and performing as many of the pretreatment steps while they are observing. In addition, supportive devices such as pillows should be placed anywhere necessary to make sure they lie flat without gaps on the treatment table. The technician should be seated at a comfortable height relative to the table, or can stand for brief periods. If they are right handed, they usually sit to the right of the customer and vice versa for most procedures. For areas where the client's hairs grow in an upward direction such as the glabellar region, the electrologist or customer may have to change positions.

Selection of the electrolysis modality

Fine vellus hair is not generally the target of electrolysis, but in desired areas containing a large amount of this type of hair, thermolysis is the modality of choice. In most cases, each application is very done very quickly at low intensity, in an attempt to avoid local irritation. Thick, rough terminal hairs are generally removed by galvanic electrolysis or the combination blend method if the area for removal is large. If the hairs are visibly wavy or curly, then the follicle is not straight either. In these cases, galvanic electrolysis which releases lye down into the dermal papilla regardless of follicle shape is the preferred method, but the blend technique can be used to speed up the removal process. For similar reasons, the galvanic and blend techniques work better on follicles that have been distorted through previous waxing or tweezing procedures. Thermolysis is only effective on hairs that are in the early growth phase.

Unless they have been distorted by previous hair removal methods, the hair follicles of Caucasians of European descent are straight. This means almost any electrolysis modality can be used unless contraindicated by some medical or skin disorder. Eastern Asians such as people of Chinese extraction have relatively small amounts of body hair, and electrolysis is usually only performed for eyebrow shaping. Individuals of African heritage with black skin usually have tightly coiled hair and bent or distorted follicles as well. This means that either galvanic electrolysis or the blend method must be used for this group in order to reach and destroy the dermal papilla region of the follicle. In addition, when other hair removal methods have been previously used on these coiled types of hair, development of ingrown hairs and pseudo-folliculitis barbae is prevalent. Individuals of Middle Eastern and Eastern Indian extraction have relatively large amounts of straight hair (unless it has been distorted), and their hair can usually be removed with thermolysis. If the technician over treats these individuals or those with black skin, unwanted excessive pigmentation can be a side effect.

Electrolysis unit

Electrolysis units are pieces of electrical equipment, which means that they must be grounded into a specifically designated outlet; they should not be exposed to sources of heat, moisture, chemicals, or airborne particles; the unit needs to sufficiently ventilated; and the cords should be not be snarled. There are some simple troubleshooting guidelines as well. If current does not appear to coming from the unit, then the power switch, outlet, fuses, and circuit breakers should be checked. If the power is on but not reaching the tip, the rheostat settings should be checked and other connections inspected. The source of the power problem can usually be identified by isolation or elimination. There is also a test bulb that can be purchased to assess whether the needle cord is intact; the test works by attaching ends to two different metal parts, the unit and the end of the probe, and pressing down on the footswitch. The bulb in the middle will light up only if the needle cord is undamaged.

Magnifying tools

Magnifying tools are useful during electrolysis. There a number of lamps that are either free-standing or can be attached somewhere in the treatment room. Lamps produce the least eyestrain for the technician, and the most frequently used magnifying lamps are circular using a circular fluorescent bulb. Common magnification ranges from 3 to 5 diopters (1 ¾ to 2 ¼ times normal). There are also several types of specialized eyewear that the technician can wear. One type called a loupe is a magnifying glass that can be worn over either eye. The point of attachment might be a clip-on addition to other glasses or a headband. Magnification is quantified in terms of the number of diopters, which can in turn be related to the power of magnification or working distance from the source. The necessary magnification range is generally 3 to 8 diopters, which translates to a working distance of between 14 and about 5 inches.

Probes

The probes used for electrolysis are really sharp needles. They are inserted into an opening, the hair follicle, instead of piercing intact skin areas. Any needle coming in contact with human skin, including an electrolysis probe, should be sterile. Completely new and unused probes that have been sterilized and prepackaged are usually used for electrolysis; a new needle is used for one treatment session with an individual client and then discarded. Alternatively, reusable probes that have been sterilized are sometimes employed. A probe diameter and length should be selected based on thickness of the hair and ability to reach into the dermal papilla portion. The type and shape of probe is chosen based on type of treatment and the skill and preference of the technician. The sizes of probes selected usually range from .002 for fine hair to .006 for very coarse hair, with .004 being the average size used.

Available probes

All probes are either one single piece of steel (or sometimes gold) that tapers at the end or a two-piece probe where a section or crimp is cut out at some point on the shank. This crimp makes the latter type of probe more flexible but also more fragile. All probes have a shank portion that is placed into the holder, a gold or steel blade that is introduced into the follicle, and an associated tip, but some probes also have a tapered section linking the shank and blade sections. Probes can be non-insulated, usually for galvanic electrolysis or the blend method, or insulated with a plastic coating on the exterior except in the tip area. The insulated probes are ideal for thermolysis because they direct the heat to the tip of the probe and the base of the hair follicle.

In general there are three different shapes of probes, tapered, cylindrical, or bulbous (a small bulb at the tip). The lye pattern that develops and aids in destruction is affected by the shape of the probe and the presence of insulation. For example, non-insulated probes distribute lye along the whole probe in the galvanic technique precluding the use of the tapered version which would concentrate most lye in the upper layers and not the base of the follicle. Bulbous needles are more difficult to insert but theoretically can concentrate more lye at the tip. Cylindrical probes can be used for all electrolysis techniques because of the even distribution of electrical current. Tapered probes are preferred for thermolysis.

<u>Forceps</u>

Forceps are critical instruments for the actual hair removal after electrolysis. They touch human blood and other bodily fluids; therefore, they have to be sterilized between uses. Thus, the forceps selected must be able to endure recurrent sterilization procedures, generally autoclaving or some chemical process. Consequently, most forceps for post-electrolysis are made of steel, and some are also electroplated at the tip area with diamond grains to grasp the hair better. There are a wide variety of shapes and lengths available, but in general the tip should be very sharp and the length should be determined by the ability of the technician to maneuver it quickly for hair removal. The technician can usually repair and sharpen forceps themselves, either by smoothing them with a stone or sandpaper.

<u>Advantages and disadvantages</u>

Electrolysis is at present the only technique approved by the Food and Drug Administration that permanently removes hair. It can be used effectively on all colors, types, and shapes of hair, on all skin types and ethnicities, and in all areas of the body with two exceptions. These exceptions are the interior portions of the nose and the ear. The technique is appropriate in any situation in which there is unwanted hair, and individual hairs are removed which is a big advantage in some cases over other methods of hair removal. The downsides of electrolysis center around its cost, the greater amount of time involved (including multiple treatments that may take several years to finish), and the possibility of pain and swelling after treatment. Clients need to adhere to certain rules about use of temporary measures to remove hair themselves, because hair needs to grow between treatments and only shaving or trimming are allowed. Medical and skin conditions need to be evaluated before treatment.

<u>Avoiding contamination</u>

Every effort should be made in the days following an electrolysis treatment to avoid contamination of the area. During electrolysis, bacteria in the hair follicle are actually killed, but the follicle takes several days to heal. If microorganisms are introduced during that time, they can spread and form pimples in the area. This contamination can be amplified by touching the area with unwashed hands or other hairs, using contaminated face creams or other makeup, and spreading the microorganisms by washing the area with water. Contamination of the area can be prevented by topical antiseptic use, temporary cleansing with unscented cleansers or germicidal soaps, application of antibiotic creams, and using only new clean or preferably no makeup. Scalp hair should not be washed for several days and it should be kept away from the facial area if treated. Tanning procedures should be avoided throughout the treatment period. Hair bleaching can safely be performed about 2 days post-electrolysis.

Re-growth

If electrolysis was not optimally performed, there can be re-growth of hairs after the procedure. Common reasons for this to occur include poor insertion technique that does not extend far enough, inadequate current applied in terms of power or period of insertion, or use of the wrong technique. In regards to the latter reason, thermolysis alone is ineffective in destroying distorted follicles. If a client has used any method at home besides trimming or shaving, the percentage of actively growing and visible hairs will be depressed. In addition, it often falsely appears that re-growth has occurred, particularly after initial treatment sessions, because many follicles are in the resting telogen phase, and new growing anagen phase hairs eventually push out of the follicle.

Deep brain stimulator implants

A deep brain stimulator (DBS) implant is a device embedded in the brain of patients who experience trembling, such as in Parkinson's disease. The metal parts and leads on the device can get too hot when any type of diathermy treatment is performed in the area. The alternating current in the thermolysis method generates a great deal of heat. In fact, this is the primary basis for its effectiveness. Therefore, while at present thermolysis units are not specifically prohibited for use in these DBS patients by the Food and Drug Administration, it is better to use the galvanic method in these individuals to avoid possible problems.

Electricity

Electricity is energy generated by the stream of negatively charged particles called electrons along a route or circuit; these electrons orbit around the nucleus of atoms. The material for this pathway must be a conductor that allows the flow of electrons, such as most metals but also salt solutions and even the human body. In electrolysis, the electrolysis needle, typically made of stainless steel, is the conductor. On the other hand, insulators resist the flow of these electrons; generally insulators are inert substances like glass or rubber. The hair does conduct electricity but rather poorly. For electrolysis techniques, electric currents are either applied continuously in one direction (direct current) such as in galvanic electrolysis, or alternating between two opposing directions (alternating current) such as in thermolysis.

Electrical terms

Electricity or electrical current is defined in terms of its force or rate of flow, termed the ampere or more often the milliampere (.001 ampere), which is usually controlled by an instrument called a rheostat. The amount of resistance in the system is quantified by a unit called the ohm, and related to the ohm is another unit called the volt. The volt is defined as the amount of force required to send one ampere of current through a resistance of 1 ohm. These terms are related to a law of physics called Ohm's law that asserts that electric current generated is directly proportional to voltage applied and inversely correlated with the amount of resistance or number of ohms. The actual electrical power or work is defined by the watt, which is one ampere applied across one volt of resistance.

Electrical devices

Electronic devices are added to equipment including those involved in electrolysis methods that either change direct current to alternating current (a rectifier), or vice versa (a converter). The voltage or resistance is usually standardized for various regions (usually 110 volts in the United States) and can be modified with a transformer. Resistance (ohms) is inherently related to the type of conductor, with metals such as steel or copper offering the least resistance. Wattage calibration can be measured by externally connecting a light bulb. In addition, safety mechanisms such as fuses or circuit breakers are included to cut off electric current when it is too much.

Thermolysis

Thermolysis employs alternating current in the form of high frequency waves such as the radio wave, microwave, or shortwave. This current is generated by a machine called an oscillator, which increases the wave frequencies back and forth. In the United States, the frequencies permitted have been restricted by the Federal Communications Commission to commonly used 13.56 megahertz (cycles per second) or twice or three times that frequency. A probe connected to the current source is put down the hair follicle, where vibrations and heat are generated in the surrounding tissues damaging them. Most probes are insulated except at the tip so the current and heat are concentrated at the base of the follicle and the dermal papilla there. Permanent hair removal only occurs when the papilla are located close to the tip. Here current is later disseminated into the air.

Galvanic electrolysis

Galvanic electrolysis employs unidirectional or direct current of electrons. Electrons initially flow from the negatively charged cathode pole (black) of the source battery containing machine through an electrolysis needle into the hair follicle. Here ions, electrically charged atoms, are liberated from the soft tissue and react to ultimately generate hydrogen gas, chlorine gas, and most importantly sodium hydroxide (NaOH or lye). Intermediate products include sodium chloride (NaCl or salt), and the ions H^+ and OH^-. Lye is the substance that destroys tissue in the follicle. Straight, curved, and distorted follicles can be destroyed by this method. The current is then dissipated through the body and returns to the generating machine through the positively charged anode terminal (red).

The sodium hydroxide or lye generated in the hair follicle during galvanic electrolysis is a very corrosive, strong alkaline substance. For the most part, the lye remains in the hair follicle and is neutralized by nearby bodily fluids. The upper layers of the follicle are drenched in sebaceous oils that are poor conductors plus at the base of the follicle, there is also a larger relative amount of moisture. Therefore, destruction is concentrated at the follicle base. The hydrogen gas formed rises and evaporates into the air. Electrons return via the body to the anode and some hydrochloric acid (HCl) can be formed there from the chlorine gas generated and water on the skin. In general, the amount of HCl is negligible and not that irritating.

Blend method of electrolysis

In the blend method of electrolysis, galvanic electrolysis and thermolysis work together. Both a direct galvanic current and a high-frequency alternating current are delivered by the same needle to the hair follicle. The galvanic current generates caustic sodium hydroxide or lye and its effects are amplified by the heat and agitation produced by the alternating current. This means the destruction is faster and more widespread. Regardless of the depth or angle of insertion, some lye will penetrate the dermal papilla. The blend method is about four times as fast as galvanic electrolysis alone.

Kobayashi-Yamada technique

The Kobayashi-Yamada technique is a modification of other thermolysis methods. It is particularly effective with coarse terminal hair and clients who are particularly sensitive to electrical stimulation. The method uses a machine where the spark jumps a gap. Although the operating frequency is lower at 1 megahertz, the power wattage produced is several times higher. The needles are insulated and an electrically charged plate is connected to the client's skin. This method can traumatize the skin and cause scars. This means pain relief in the form of local anesthetics or cold packs needs to be available. It is a newer and more controversial technique.

Anaphoresis and cataphoresis

The overall term phoresis is the process of transmitting chemical solutions through intact skin by use of a direct current. The movement of ions through the organic material is known as iontophoresis. There are two types of phoresis. One form of phoresis, anaphoresis, introduces negatively charged ions which flow from a negative to a negative pole. This procedure is sometimes used to open up pores, dilate blood vessels and increase blood flow in an area, or activate nerve endings; it also produces the same kind of tissue softening and alkaline substances found in galvanic electrolysis. The opposite procedure, cataphoresis, introduces positive ions into the skin via a saturated roller acting as a positive electrode. This technique is sometimes used to constrict the pores and blood vessels, firm tissues, and in general soothe the area after other treatments. It may kill bacteria as well.

Relative hydration level

The relative concentration of moisture or water in layers of an individual's skin is their hydration level. Dry skin is an indication of less hydration in the lower layers of the skin, less secretion of oils into the upper layers, and less shedding of dead skin cells. This tendency increases as we age, although dry skin can occur at many times. This phenomenon is relevant to the practice of electrolysis because the water conducts the electric current while the oily portions insulate against the conduction of current. Untoward side effects such as blistering can be avoided by observing the moisture gradient of the client's skin and choosing the appropriate modality. For example, if skin that is very moist is treated with thermolysis, the heat could in theory rise to the epidermal surface.

Depth of the hair follicles

In order to establish the required treatment energy for an electrolysis procedure in a particular area, the technician initially needs to determine the average depth of the hair follicle. This is done by removing a hair under minimal energy requirements while grasping and then removing the hair with a forceps. The hair that has been removed is then held against the probe to determine how far from the tip the hair goes; this point can be assumed to be the average depth if the hair is in its growth phase. The appropriate treatment intensity can be determined by starting at a low value and increasing this until the hair releases from the shaft. In addition, visible stiffer hairs should be removed first, and the distribution of removal should be widespread, not concentrated only in one area. The emphasis should be on successful hair removal, not speed.

Scalp, back of the neck, and hairline

In general, hairs on the scalp, back of the neck, and hairline are about 3 to 5 millimeters deep. These hairs are not straight up from the skin, but usually at an angle of about 60 degrees. While most of these hairs are terminal, at the hairline some will be vellus hairs;

plus the angle can become smaller toward the temple area, around 40 degrees. The client is usually seated on the table, but may be face down for removal from the back of the neck. Hairs need to be pre-trimmed to about one quarter inch, which is easy to grasp with the forceps. The needle selected should be the same diameter as the hairs. Stronger one piece probes are preferred for scalp hair because of the relatively long sessions usually required.

Unique considerations for electrolysis

<u>Eyebrow area</u>

Since hair removal by electrolysis is permanent, a plan for the proper shaping of the eyebrow area needs to be in place before the procedure is begun. The client is usually lying down with their head supported by a pillow and tilted toward the technician, but they may be seated when the area between the eyebrows is being treated. Hairs in the eyebrow area grow at very shallow angles. At the outer edges, the angle can be from 10 to 30 degrees, while toward the glabellar region these angles can increase and even be straight up. The growth direction is generally downward, which means hairs at the top of the hairline are not usually removed. The skin in the eyebrow area is relatively thin and blood vessels are in proximity to the hair follicles there. This means that narrow flexible two-piece probes are generally indicated for use in the eyebrow area to avoid bruising. Consequently, materials such as ice and arnica montana oil should be readily available to put on the area to avoid this bruising as well.

<u>Outer ear area</u>

Only hair on the outer portion of the ear should be removed. Follicles in this region are comparatively short, about 1 to 2 ½ millimeters deep. The incline of the hairs is relatively sharp; it ranges from about 45 degrees at the visible auricle portion to virtually straight up on both sides of the tragus, which is the flap that partially covers the entrance to the inner ear. It is paramount to avoid getting anesthetic or other substances into the ear canal or auditory meatus, so they must be applied with cotton directly to the outer ear. The customer lies prone with their head supported during the removal procedures. One side of the tragus area can also be treated in a session if the head is tilted to one side.

<u>Upper and lower lip areas</u>

Electrolysis of the upper lip excites nerve endings in the area which subsequently stimulates the tear ducts causing possible tearing. Thus anesthetic preparations are usually put on the upper lip before the procedure, and the sensation is ablated after each removal by slapping the area with the forefinger. Hairs are often hard to visualize in the lip region, so commercially available preparations called follicle enhancers often need to be temporarily applied, especially for hairs that are light in color or those lacking pigmentation. Anagen hair in the lip region is not very deep, up to about 2.5 mm, and the follicles are at a very narrow incline of about 10 to 30 degrees. The client is lying down with head support, and cotton rolls are placed between the gums and lips. Removal should commence at the outside edge working inward. When the bow of the lip, called the divot, is reached, it should be manually pinched outward for better access; the growth pattern here is sort of out and downward. Treatments should address both sides equally. Further visits should not be scheduled for at least a week.

Nose

Electrolysis is rarely performed on the nose. Occasionally, people with dark hair or older individuals may develop noticeable hair growth along the apex of the nose especially near the tip. This area can be treated with electrolysis but only at very low power. This is because the area is very prone to scabbing since the hair follicles in this region are very short (about 1 millimeter) and at a very small angle to the skin (30 degrees or less). This also means that the hairs removed are in areas where a great deal of sebum or oil is being produced. The treatment of choice for hair removal on the top of the nose would be low energy thermolysis. Sneezing often occurs when either the nose or lip areas are treated.

Sideburn area

Sideburns are a complex mixture of types of hair (both terminal and vellus), follicle depth (typically 3 to 5 millimeters if actively growing), and follicle incline (anywhere from 10 to 45 degrees to the epidermis). Prior to electrolysis, the technician and customer need to establish the desired extent of removal and whether any vellus hair is to be extracted along with the terminal hairs. Before beginning the electrolysis, the hairs should be cut to about a quarter inch. The recommended protocol for removal by electrolysis is to start where the client wishes the sideburn to terminate away from the hairline. The pattern of removal is down followed by inward.

Facial hair

Facial hair is defined as any hair from right below the eye area down to the jaw line. Typically, most hair in this region is of the lightly pigmented vellus type. However, undesirable pigmented terminal hair can develop on the face, particularly in females of Middle-Eastern extraction or in Caucasians or others who have taken certain medications or had hair removed in the area by non-permanent techniques. If electrolysis is performed on facial hair, an equalized look with no bald spots must be maintained. The pattern of removal is from the cheekbone area working from the nose to the side of the face and then proceeding downward. Precision is paramount because if the destruction is incomplete, the remaining hair can become an irritant and cause pustules, ingrown hairs, or increased pigmentation to occur.

Chin area

Hair in the chin area can be a complex mixture of relatively nonpigmented vellus hairs and visible, colored, rough terminal hairs. The hair follicles may be distorted from previous non-permanent procedures, their angles vary widely up to sticking straight out, and many individuals have a large amount of sebum production in the chin area. In the chin area, it is difficult to pull some of the hairs out because their sheath is very thick, and the stronger one piece probes are often used. If electrolysis is performed on the terminal hairs, it is usually done at a relatively high intensity. Destruction of the sebaceous gland in this region is acceptable, even preferred, because the tendency for pustule development is abated. The preferred method of removal for the chin would be galvanic electrolysis or possibly the blend method if there are many hairs to be excised. The customer should shave a few days before the procedure is there are a lot of hairs to remove.

Throat region

The throat region is very susceptible to bruising, particularly in relatively hairy females who are overweight. This tendency is probably due to an endocrine imbalance, and the bruising can be minimized through use of post-treatment pressure, icing the area, and application of oils or arnica Montana cream. Men may develop densely packed, rough, deeply rooted hairs in the throat area due to repeated shaving of the region. The hairs can only be removed with high intensity treatments, which can lead to tissue destruction and subsequent lesions. Therefore, it is important to space out the areas treated in these men. Shaving should be done a few days prior to treatment if there are many hairs to remove. The angle of the hairs in the throat area can range from very shallow (10 degrees) to much greater.

Arms, hands, and knuckles

Hairs on the arms should be shaved before electrolysis treatment to expose the relatively low percentage of anagen phase hairs in this region. The follicle angle is rather shallow, but it can be much steeper if the arms have been previously waxed. The arm is supported with a pillow, and the entire area misted with antiseptic. The hands and knuckles are prone to lesions after treatment. This is particularly true for the knuckles because the hairs there stick almost straight up and are very rough and difficult to remove. It is difficult to keep this area disinfected post-treatment. Therefore, the client should be instructed to refrain from using any products containing dyes or fragrance, and should wash their hands periodically.

Genital area

Performing electrolysis in the genital area presents a situation that must be handled very discreetly and professionally. The client should be offered disposable underwear to change into privately. The area needs to be isolated and draped. The customer is either prone or is partially reclined. After thorough cleansing, the area is usually externally anesthetized to dull the pain and permit faster procedures. Either thermolysis or the blend methods are recommended for speed of use. The galvanic or blend modalities can interfere with intrauterine devices if present. Hairs can present at angles from 20 to 60 degrees and they are very coarse; they usually need to be cut off to manageable levels before treatment. As low a treatment level as possible should be determined and utilized to minimize the possibility of scabbing. Ingrown hairs should be released but not excised. The pattern of hair development in the genital area is toward the center and downward, which means the electrologist begins at the outer edge of the top of the area and works down along the bikini line generally.

<u>Buttocks, legs, feet and toes</u>

Both the buttocks and legs have relatively thicker and softer flesh than some other areas of the body. Consequently, the skin may need to be stretched during the electrolysis procedure to gain proper access to the follicle, especially at the knee. The follicle angle can also be very shallow (sometimes only 10 degrees) in both these regions as well as on parts of the feet and toes. The main issue with electrolysis in the buttocks region is privacy and appropriate draping of the area; the client is face down and the hair growth pattern is down and toward the inside of the buttocks. The primary consideration for leg procedures is that the limbs should be previously exfoliated to get rid of dead skin; the growth pattern is complex. Conditions affecting the circulatory system preclude removal on the feet and toes, and this is also an area susceptible to scabbing and readily exposed to pathogens after the procedure.

Pattern of hair growth

<u>Chest, breast and areola areas</u>

The pattern of hair on the human chest is intricate. At the top of the chest, hairs tend to grow upward toward the chin. Near the clavicle bone (about shoulder blade level), the hairs usually develop horizontally toward the center, and then the direction of proliferation is more downward toward the sternum or breastbone. Shaving a few days before treatment is recommended to expose only actively growing hairs. On the actual breast and dark central areola area, the pattern of hair growth is usually very erratic necessitating careful observation before removal. Hair can be extracted from the areola region, but there a few unique considerations. The area is sensitive, no anesthetics can be applied to the areola, and there can be several hairs originating from the same follicle. Only one hair should be removed from an individual follicle in a single session to avoid tissue injury and infection

<u>Axilla</u>

The axilla is the armpit region, and the pattern of hair growth is not only complex but may differ between the two axillae. The technician must determine the removal direction by observation. The armpit area is very sensitive, and pretreatment with topical anesthetics is suggested. It is also a breeding ground for bacteria. This means most female clients use antiperspirants or deodorants which must be cleaned off before the procedure. Shaving a few days before electrolysis is recommended to isolate anagen phase hairs because in the armpit only about a quarter of hairs are actively growing. Removal in this area does not extend far enough into the skin to affect the lymph nodes. Any electrolysis treatment mode can be utilized. The hairs can be very coarse so usually a single shaft probe is preferred unless the growth pattern warrants use of a more flexible needle.

Abdominal region

Hairs on the abdomen may be any combination of vellus and terminal hairs. If only terminal hairs are found, the abdomen should be shaved several days before electrolysis. If vellus hair is present, only the unwanted terminal hairs should be separately cut down at that time. Hairs in the abdominal region generally grow at very shallow angles and are relatively long. The pattern of proliferation is toward the center of the body and in the direction of the navel. For the treatment, the patient lies down, and the technician isolates the area by use of drapes.

Post-electrolysis

After electrolysis, the probe is removed from the unit and either thrown out in the sharps container or put in the isolyser for later sterilization. Other parts should be prepared for disinfecting procedures and the unit turned off. There are a variety of post-treatment lotions and gels available, but they must be applied in ways that do not expose the sterile hair follicle to bacteria on the skin or elsewhere (including from the product's jar). Typically, this means applying these substances sparingly with a spatula, cotton balls, or a washcloth; alternatively ice or cold packs can be applied. Shampooing cannot be done, and other hair products should not be used for at least a day. Any scabs that have formed should be moistened with topical antibiotics and allowed to naturally fall off. Exposure to ultraviolet rays of the sun should be avoided or at least kept in check through use of high SPF sunscreens.

Probes and forceps

Coordinating the use of the probe for electrolysis and the forceps for actual hair removal or epilation is a matter of personal preference and repeated practice. The one required constant is that the electrologist should control the probe with their dominant hand (for example, right hand for a right-handed individual). The probe is gripped and maneuvered by the thumb and forefinger and assisted by the other fingers. The forceps can be held in the same hand and used for subsequent removal. Another technique is to keep the forceps in the non-dominant hand and epilate either with that hand or by transfer of the forceps to the dominant hand. Stretching of the client's skin between the two hands in order to open up and release the hair facilitates a proper insertion, and this can best be accomplished with the one-handed technique. The use of two different hands for insertion and epilation can still provide a good stretch with practice, but it is hard to maintain the stretch when forceps are being transferred.

One-handed insertion technique

In the one-handed or forehand insertion technique, the rigid body of the needle holder is held between the thumb and index finger of the dominant hand. The forceps is slid in between the thumb and the probe holder with the pointed end facing outwards and held in place with the fourth and fifth fingers. When inserting the probe, the middle finger is pressed against the client's skin to provide stability and direct the needle. Then the electrolysis insertion is performed by straightening and flexing the index finger and thumb to move the probe into and out of the follicle. After withdrawal at the exact same angle as insertion, the needle holder is moved to between the second and third fingers, and the sharp end of the forceps is grasped between the thumb and index finger. The forceps tip is used to pull the hair out at approximately a 90 degree angle to the shaft in the direction of hair growth, and then the probe and forceps are returned to their original positions for another insertion.

Backhand variation

The backhand variation of a one-handed or forehand insertion is useful in areas with hairs growing in various directions because it allows the technician to remove hairs that are oriented away from them without moving. The probe and forceps are held in dominant hand in the same manner as for a forehand insertion, but the wrist is bent enough to allow the knuckle of the middle finger to lie on the client's skin. This allows for insertion and removal of the probe in the opposing direction. The wrist is then uncurled and the forceps maneuvered into position to pull out the hair.

Stretching techniques

When insertion is performed with only one hand, the other hand is used to stretch the client's skin in order to provide a tauter surface and wider follicle opening for insertion. Sometimes a two-fingered stretch is done; here the thumb and index finger of the non-dominant hand are used to pull the skin in opposition to the insertion site. More often, a three-way stretch is performed. In the latter technique, generally the thumb and forefinger are positioned parallel to the insertion site and both used to provide a mild stretch, while at the same time the middle finger of the dominant probe-controlling hand assists the stretch. The hair is electrolyzed and removed in a perpendicular orientation to the two fingers on the non-dominant hand for either technique.

Acceptable insertion

There are three generally accepted probe insertion techniques for electrolysis. In the first, called the preelectrolysis epilation technique, or PEET, the technician pulls out the hair before then inserting the probe and directing the current into the follicle to destroy the dermal papilla. In the next procedure, the probe and current are inserted first with the hair in place, the hair pulled out, and then the electrolysis procedure is repeated in the empty follicle; this is called postepilation reentry technique or PERT. In the final technique, standard electrolysis is done, but the probe is left in the follicle while the hair is plucked using the other hand, and then a second wave of energy is applied for further destruction. This postepilation sustained entry technique, or PEST, can only be mastered using a two-handed procedure. The needle should always be inserted in the reverse direction to hair proliferation and below the hair in parallel to it.

Incorrect insertion

One common undesired effect of an incorrect probe insertion is the drawing of the client's blood. This can occur for a number of reasons, primarily because the probe has been inserted too deeply or at an incorrect angle to direct it down the hair follicle. In the latter case, the side of the hair shaft is generally touched; the hair then breaks off at that point and tissue destruction can occur. Insertions that are too shallow are more common, however, and thus the papilla is not destroyed. If modalities that produce lye are used, this is not a huge issue because the sodium hydroxide will still eventually reach the dermal papilla. Sometimes the insertion is inserted too close to the side of the hair follicle. Every effort should be made to insert the probe cleanly and accurately.

Carpel tunnel syndrome

The most common job-related problem an electrologist might develop is carpel tunnel syndrome. This syndrome is characterized by weakness and pain in the hands and wrists and usually running up the forearm. It results from recurring use of the bones, ligaments, and tendons in this carpal region. Initially the overused tendons become swollen and inflamed, and eventually the median nerve is affected. The individual is then incapacitated for up to 6 weeks by surgical procedures, use of a wrist brace, or other therapies. Prevention of carpal tunnel syndrome is essential for the electrologist. Finger and wrist exercises, stretching, and massages are helpful.

Thermolysis

Thermolysis uses a high-frequency alternating current of sound waves at a rate of 30 megahertz, or 30 million cycles per second. These waves are conducted through the air. When thermolysis is applied to the hair follicle, it sets up a magnetic field, which in turn stimulates the atoms in the surrounding tissue to be constantly attracted and repelled generating heat. If the thermolysis is performed correctly, the temperature generated at the probe tip in the region of the dermal papilla is about 160^0F. Temperatures above 110^0F will cause destruction of the tissues or electrocoagulation. Higher temperatures can cause the tissues to dry (greater than 212^0F) or burn and scar (greater than 240^0F).

Thermolysis machines
Thermolysis machines are classified according to their method of operation, either manually, semi-manually, or some type of computerized machine. If a manual machine is used, all settings are selected by the operating technician who also controls the length of time the current is applied by the use of either a foot pedal or a button located on the probe. Semi-manual machines are similar but include an automatic timer to control the time interval of the actual thermolysis. Currently there are a variety of computerized machines, and many of these can be set to perform a number

of techniques including thermolysis. Capabilities of these apparatuses can include automatic operation (no foot pedal), data storage, and a flash feature. This latter flash feature is useful in assuaging the client's pain because the nerve endings controlling pain are initially "flashed" or destabilized before the real treatment energy is delivered.

Waves generated

The waves generated within the follicle during thermolysis are affected by the density, intensity, and duration of current applied; the depth of insertion; and the moisture gradient. Density refers to the number of electrons that are being delivered by the conducting needle and it is a constant number. The amount of heat generated is related to the length of time the current is employed, or duration, which typically ranges between 0.05 and 0.15 of a second, as well as the intensity of the current, which is generally expressed in amperes (the magnitude of energy generated by one volt of potential difference and dissipating one watt of power) or milliamperes. Intensity can also be set as a percentage of that available on the thermolysis machine. The depth of probe insertion affects the wave pattern and heat generation at the tip; the least heat is actually produced with a correct deep insertion into the papilla because the current is less concentrated in that area while being dispersed over a larger portion of tissue. In moist areas, the temperature can increase and the heat can move up to the skin surface and cause lesions.

Selection of probes

Probes that are insulated are preferred for the thermolysis modality because they direct the current, heat, and tissue destruction to the tip of the probe and hopefully the dermal papilla region. This intense focus on the tip means that the treatment energy needs to be set lower than when using no insulated probes. The best type of construction for these insulated probes is a single shaft tapered probe because these types are very strong and they can pinpoint the desired area, but cylindrically shaped flexible two-piece probes are useful as well. Tapered and cylindrical shaped probes that are not insulated will discharge electrons along the entire needle instead of targeting the papilla and are therefore less desirable. There is another type of probe called bulbous which has a small bulb on the end; this type is typically harder to insert and offers no advantage. The diameter of the probe should approximate that of the hairs to be epilated.

Advantages and disadvantages

Thermolysis is a relatively rapid and easy technique to perform. It can be used to remove not only terminal but also vellus hairs with minimal incidence of re-growth if performed correctly. Thermolysis is also effective on fine terminal hairs and those with shallower growth angles. It does not produce marks on the skin as in galvanic electrolysis because there is no attached positive pole. However, thermolysis is less effective on the rougher terminal hairs and on distorted follicles. This is because the tip and heat generated both really need to be directed into the dermal papilla region, and less current is generally applied. Any condition precluding other types of hair removal contraindicates the use of thermolysis as well. In addition, this technique is usually ineffectual on the curved follicles of individuals of African descent.

Pretreatment procedures

The pretreatment procedures to perform before thermolysis center on (1) selection of the correct modality on the machinery and testing the equipment, (2) preparation of the client, (3) probe selection and sterile insertion of the needle into the probe, and (4) setting the machine dials to deliver the correct treatment energy. Once the thermolysis mode has been chosen, the current flow can be confirmed by monitoring the light indicator or use of a light bulb tester. Client preparation, probe selection, and sterile techniques have been previously discussed. The manufacturer of the equipment will usually indicate preferred settings for density, intensity and duration; the treatment energy is a product of the intensity times the duration.

Epilation process

During thermolysis, the epilation process is begun by slipping the probe into the chosen hair follicle. The previously selected current is then applied by depressing the foot pedal (this step may vary on a computerized machine). Current is either removed by releasing pressure from the foot pedal on a manual apparatus or cut off automatically by a timer in other versions. The probe is slid out and the hair removed with the forceps. If removal is difficult, then either the intensity or time of current application must be increased for greater subsequent treatment energy or insertion technique must be checked. A single follicle can be used treated up to three times. Once these parameters have been adjusted to allow easy hair removal, a working treatment energy is obtained that should be effective for removing other hairs. During the treatment, parameters can still be changed if necessary for a smooth removal. When using a manual machine, each part of the process (insertion, application of current, stopping the flow of current, and probe removal) should be of equal duration, about 2 seconds.

<u>Over treatment</u>

The most common effect of over treatment during thermolysis is a condition termed "high-frequency blowout". In this situation, the treatment energy delivered was too much, and regardless of whether the cause was excessive intensity or length of application, extreme amounts of heat are generated. The excessive heat is enough to bring the tissues to a boiling point. The steam generated prevents conduction so the current ascends to the skin surface. Fragments of tissue can stick to the probe causing a crackling sound, and lesions can form on the surface of the skin.

Pulsing and flashing techniques

Pulsing is a technique in which current is used in a series of short bursts instead of a longer continuous period. The method is usually employed in very sensitive skin regions. On a manual machine, the foot pedal is tapped, but other machines can be programmed to deliver pulses of current. In flashing, a high-density current is applied very quickly, up to about a half a second. The heat generated is intensely focused into the dermal papilla. This technique is really only effective on finer, straight hairs with shallow follicle angles. This has also been called the rapid flash technique. Its advantage is that the nerve endings have less time to register the associated pain, but its disadvantage is the relative high rate of hair re-growth.

Galvanic electrolysis

In galvanic electrolysis, a direct current is unidirectionally applied. In any type of true electrolysis, chemicals are separated through the use of an electric current. In galvanic electrolysis for permanent hair removal, in the hair follicle water (chemical

- 69 -

formula H_2O) and salt or sodium chloride (NaCl) are pulled apart and rearranged into molecules of hydrogen gas, chlorine gas, and the most importantly, sodium hydroxide or lye (NaOH). The galvanic machine is turned on, and the intensity and flow are set with the rheostat and milliampere meter gauge respectively. For this technique, the client needs to hold a moistened attachment coming from the positive electrode to complete the circuit. When the technician presses down on the foot pedal, direct current (DC) is discharged from the negatively charged pole through the probe tip into the follicle and eventually out through the individual to the positive electrode. The lye produced in the follicle should theoretically destroy the dermal papilla tissue.

Advantages and disadvantages

Hair removed by the galvanic electrolysis technique rarely grows back. This is because even if the insertion was inaccurate, the caustic sodium hydroxide or lye generated still trickles down into the papilla region destroying it. This also means that hairs in distorted or curved follicles can be effectively removed, and the lye continues to destroy tissue after the probe is removed. The biggest disadvantage of galvanic electrolysis is that current is generally applied for a longer period of time, and the client may therefore experience more pain. The interaction between the client and the technician has to be well defined because the customer needs to remain relatively still for protracted periods and they must hold the positive electrode. The lye that remains in the follicles after the process can cause irritation, and the hydrochloric acid that can be generated on the positive end can result in lasting dark marking of the skin. The latter condition, known as tattooing, should not occur if the circuit has been correctly set up.

Success rate of hair removal

In galvanic electrolysis, tissue destruction is caused by the lye generated. The strength of the lye solution is greatest near the probe, and it diminishes with increasing distance from the probe. If the dermal papilla is too far from the critical zone of effectiveness, it will not be destroyed. The density of the current, or the concentration of electron flow, is directly related to lye production. The treatment energy is the product of the current intensity and the time the current is applied; here the amount of lye produced is being measured. Changing either the intensity or duration can affect the treatment energy. Typical current intensities are between 0.3 and 0.7 milliamperes (ma) with a single probe and lower if

- 70 -

multiple needles are used, usually between 0.08 and 0.12 ma. Current is usually applied for about 30 seconds to a minute, but the application can be considerably longer, up to 3 or 5 minutes for single or multiple probes respectively. Treatment energy required is generally much higher for terminal hairs than vellus ones. Insertion depth is generally not crucial. The probe type must be carefully selected as well.

Shocking

Shocking refers to any type of discomfort experienced by the customer during the galvanic procedure. During the electrolysis, if excessive current is employed to the hair follicle, the individual can undergo a generalized shocking, generally a tingling or burning feeling. When a multiple-needle machine is being utilized, the current being delivered to each follicle is generally less, but each small effect can be bundled into a mass effect type of shocking. In addition, an abrupt jolt can be felt sometimes when the current is switched on or off; this problem is rarely observed today because newer machines have been designed to progressively change the level of current.

Probe choice

The selection of an insulated versus a non-insulated probe for galvanic electrolysis is controversial. Although an insulated probe more effectively focuses the energy and lye production into the probe tip and dermal papilla respectively, it does not destroy the sebaceous glands because the upper 2/3 of the probe is sheathed in plastic. Some experts feel that these oil-producing glands should be destroyed in addition to the actual hair removal. Nevertheless, insulated probes are popular, but should be used with lower intensities. The bulbous shape is very effective in delivering the greatest amount of lye to the papilla region regardless of whether the probe is insulated or not. The preferred type of needle is the noninsulated cylindrical probe because the caustic lye is evenly distributed in the follicle so both the papilla and oil glands are damaged.

Unique considerations

In galvanic electrolysis, a complete electric circuit traveling in one direction through the client's body is set up. Any type of metallic entity worn by or inserted into the body of the individual undergoing galvanic electrolysis can divert the path of electrons. The latter can range from pins inserted at various joints to implanted pacemakers, dental work, skull plates and intrauterine devices (IUDs). Both electrodes need to be placed in areas that are distant from any such metal devices. In addition, the current should not circulate through the pelvic region, especially if the client is pregnant or wearing an IUD, and thermolysis is the method of choice for removal in the abdominal or bikini areas in these cases. The handheld electrode should always be placed in the same hand as the side of removal for the upper lip because otherwise the current will circulate throughout the mouth and produce a metallic sensation there.

Iontophoresis

Iontophoresis is the movement of ions through biological tissues by use of an electric current. In galvanic electrolysis, this occurs because rollers attached to either the negative or positive pole are saturated with some type of solution that conducts the electrical current. After the galvanic technique, the current on the client's skin can be redistributed using a roller to a larger surface area by cataphoresis. This is done by attaching a carbon or steel roller to the anode or positive pole of the machine and applying about 2 ma of current through moistened gauze. Cataphoresis can kill bacteria in addition to decreasing redness on the skin surface.

Blend method

The blend method of electrolysis combines both galvanic electrolysis and thermolysis in the same procedure. Both the direct current of the galvanic method and the alternating current of the thermolysis are applied either at the same time or in succession to combine the caustic destructive effects of the DC with the heat-producing qualities of the AC. The result is a method with the potential to be much faster and thorough because the heat from thermolysis accelerates and potentiates the chemical reaction in which sodium hydroxide or lye is liberated during the galvanic electrolysis. Hot lye is much more corrosive than the same substance at lower temperatures.

Epilators

Currently available blend epilators range from those that are manually controlled to ones that are either partially or entirely controlled automatically. In a manual blend epilator, the technician controls the administration of the two types of currents, galvanic DC and thermolysis AC, by use of foot pedals. This method is inherently more variable than other types, but allows for individual adaptations. Semi-automatic machines allow the operator to set some parameters such as duration or intensity before starting the procedure, but some manual component such as foot pedal use may be retained. Other machines are fully automated; in this case, once the hair type is entered, all other parameters are set up automatically. The more automated machines usually include other conveniences like hair counters. Unfortunately, the more automated machines do not provide many ways to individualize the hair removal.

Working point

On a blend type epilator, the machine is warmed up and the client is attached to the positive electrode. First the working point for the thermolysis portion of the procedure is determined by manipulating the machine at relatively low intensities for up to 10 seconds until a combination that will release the hair is reached. Then the units of lye for the type of hair are determined. A similar intensity versus duration sequence is done using the galvanic direct current. The galvanic setting should be the calculated as the theoretical upper limit for the type of hair divided in the number of seconds the high frequency determination was done. In other words, the number of theoretical lye units (ma/sec) is divided by HF time (sec), yielding the number of milliamperes to use for the galvanic portion.

Advantages and disadvantages

The main advantage of the blend method of hair removal is its speed of use coupled with its augmented efficacy. Any hairs that have curved follicles can be removed. This is possible because the hot lye seeps into the papilla regardless of depth of insertion. Hairs at all growth stages can generally be detached, and the method is effective on a variety of types of hairs in many areas of the body. Because of the more complex nature of the blend method, however, it is trickier to learn and control, and the potential for adverse side effects from use of too high treatment energies exists.

Considerations

If the blend technique is not properly controlled, various skin lesions can develop on the surface. Obviously, these types of side effects need to be avoided in the face area.

Therefore, when working on the face, the electrologist needs to deactivate the alternating or "master" current before there is any evidence of the ascendance of gases, debris, or other heating products up the follicle. In general, this means the level of AC should be in the moderate range and the duration of this alternating current is about 6 to 20 seconds. High frequencies should not be used on the facial area. On the other hand, lesion formation is less of a concern when epilating other body areas, and typically in those regions short bursts (2 seconds or less) of high frequency alternating current are coupled with a couple bouts of concurrent direct galvanic current. The client should shave these areas a few days before the procedure to expose anagen phase hairs and facilitate a quicker removal.

Unit of lye

A unit of lye has been defined as the amount of sodium hydroxide produced by the direct current during galvanic electrolysis of 1/10 milliampere flowing for 1 second. By the galvanic method alone, the number of lye units typically required for removal ranges from 15 units for vellus hairs up to 80 units for the extremely deep terminal hairs of a man's beard. However, with the blend method, the heating of the AC from the thermolysis portion can make each theoretical lye unit on average 4 times more effective, especially if high frequencies are used. Therefore, these adaptations are considered in determination of the working point for the blend method.

The upper limits in terms of lye units for the galvanic portion of a blend epilation are 15 lye units for vellus hair, 30 units for terminal hairs in the facial and arm regions, 60 units for deeper terminal hairs in females and the back and shoulder areas of males, and 80 units for coarse beards. These 4 distinctions translate into typical galvanic durations of 8, 10, 12 and 15 seconds respectively, and usual galvanic intensities of 0.25, 0.35, 0.45, and 0.55 milliamperes respectively. For the thermolysis part of the blend method, the four types of hair classifications generally translate into durations of 0.2 seconds up to from 0.3 to a half second and intensity percentages from 5% on the low end to 10 to 15% on the end depending on the type of hair.

Theory of neuronal blockade

The theory of neuronal blockage asserts that initially applying only one of the modalities of the blend method, either the galvanic electrolysis or the thermolysis, impairs the nerve endings in the area and lessens the pain experienced when the other process is subsequently applied. For this reason, sequential rather than concurrent application of the two processes is often preferred for hair removal by the blend method. Galvanic electrolysis in usually done first (but not always) because the lye produced bleeds into the follicle and opens it up regardless of its configuration or possible blockage.

Hair follicles

The thermolysis part of the blend method agitates and heats up the lye produced by galvanism in the blend method. The speed of the chemical reaction producing this sodium hydroxide in bodily tissues is increased two-fold for approximately every 22 degrees Fahrenheit elevation in the temperature range utilized, making the blend technique very fast. The high-frequency AC current of the thermolysis portion coagulates or changes the tissues into a more porous or permeable consistency, which allows for quick absorption of the lye generated during the galvanic electrolysis part. Agitation in the follicle from the high-frequency AC further augments the absorption rate.

Adverse side effects

Unfortunately, the potential for adverse side effects is increased with the blend method. These untoward effects can include steam production in the follicle which forces current and tissue fragments back upwards ("high-frequency blowout") resulting in possible skin lesions, or trapping of gases in the follicle or surrounding tissues in sequential protocols where galvanic electrolysis is performed first. This latter condition can occur if the probe in the later thermolysis portion blocks gas escape. In addition, appropriate probe combinations can differ from single technique removals and recommendations should be followed in order to assure easy removal without side effects.

Pre-shaving

Shaving is a temporary way to manage undesired hair growth without stimulating rapid or coarse re-growth. If areas that are to undergo some method of electrolysis are pre-shaved one to three days before treatment, primarily growing anagen phase hairs will be exposed for removal. This is the desired effect since it is impossible to prevent re-growth of hairs during the resting telogen phase. Follicles containing telogen hairs tend to be shorter than ones with anagen hairs. The papilla in these resting phase shafts are usually missed during electrolysis or the follicle is actually often pierced. Anagen hairs will glide out of the follicle easily at appropriate treatment energies whereas telogen hairs will not, and side effects such as the formation of surface crusts or bruises are minimized if only growing hairs are properly removed.

Electrolysis insertion

Initially, the electrolysis needle or probe should be slid into the follicle beneath the hair in the correct angle against the path of hair growth. If the skin surface forms a slight depression or dimple, then either the insertion angle is wrong or the diameter of the needle is too wide. At that point, the technician should either draw back on the probe or pull it out and start again if the dimpling occurs at the onset or if the needle needs to be changed. Otherwise, the electrologist will feel a resistance at the point where the follicle is pierced. The customer will feel pain, and they should be encouraged to communicate this to the technician to avoid errors. Removal with the forceps should be at the same correct angle in the direction of hair growth.

Regardless of the treatment modality, the combination of factors (intensity, duration, energy, angle of insertion, needle size, etc.) selected for the electrolysis should result in easy removal of the hairs. All equipment must be used with caution, especially the needles and forceps; this is important not only for general safety but also to avoid skin surface side effects. It is essential to make sure the current is shut off before pulling out the needle. Moisture on the skin surface attracts the current so exposure of the probe to that wetness can affect the treatment energy or inadvertently activate the current. The same types of hairs should be removed before changing treatment parameters, and the removal pattern should be widespread with no adjacent hairs excised during one treatment session. In addition to the proper insertion techniques, working points and insertion depths need to be adjusted when necessary to prevent the need for double insertions or removal of hairs without attached bulbs.

Sequence of procedures

Before the electrolysis procedure, all equipment should be cleaned and turned on. Sterilization or disinfection procedures should be followed for all equipment, and the technician needs to thoroughly wash their hands. The sterile needle should be inserted into the probe holder with sterile forceps. The client's skin should be cleaned and dried. The positive electrode should be prepared and attached to the customer if appropriate for the modality. Machine settings are adjusted according to the observed hair type to be removed, and the selected electrolysis procedure is performed. Afterwards, protective needle caps are replaced, all disposable equipment is discarded in the sharps or biohazard containers, and reusable equipment to be sterilized is appropriately dispersed to those facilities. Aftercare for the client needs to be performed. The positive electrode should be cleaned and dried, documentation should be completed, the table should be changed, and the technician washes their hands again. At the end of a shift, the Electrologist should turn off all equipment, clean the magnifier and other apparatuses, and finish any recordkeeping.

Client aftercare procedures post-electrolysis are minimal. Cleansing the skin area for electrolysis is often performed before the procedure and sometimes afterwards as well in order to get rid of superficial bacteria; a common cleanser is Savlon (primarily chlorhexidine gluconate). If the area is red or irritated, cool water can be splashed on the surface or applied with a washcloth or witch hazel or hydrocortisone creams may be applied. If these solutions or creams are used, clean swabs need to be used for each application to avoid contamination of the bottle or tube. It is also crucial to remind the client not to scratch or chafe the area in any way, not to use any fragrance or makeup, and to avoid exposure to the sun until the inflammation abates.

Sterilization procedures

Any object that actually is inserted into tissue or is exposed to blood or other bodily fluids is considered to be critical. These objects must be sterilized before and after use, and they include the epilating needle and equipment used to extract blackheads. The most commonly used methods of sterilization are steam heat (autoclave for example), dry heat, ethylene oxide gas, or immersion in 2% glutaraldehyde solutions.

Occasionally chlorine dioxide or 6% hydrogen peroxide are used for sterilization (6 hours each) but both can oxidize and rust certain chemicals such as copper and brass.

The same types of procedures employed for critical equipment should be utilized for sterilization of semi critical objects that touch mucous membranes or broken skin, such as the machine electrodes and tweezers. For this category of equipment, acceptable procedures also include detergent cleaning followed by boiling at 75 degrees Centigrade for a half hour, or immersion in high concentrations of sodium hypochlorite solutions (corrosive for metals). Equipment that only comes in contact with intact skin, like the machinery or magnifier, is considered non-critical. In this case, disinfection to lower microbial exposure is sufficient. Disinfectants include sodium hypochlorite in the same or lower concentrations as above, 70 to 90% alcohol (either ethyl or isopropyl), or detergent solutions with phenolic, iodophor or quaternary ammonium formulations.

Manual galvanic electrolysis

Manual or semi-manual galvanic electrolysis machines use either foot pedals or hand buttons to activate the current. The machine should be turned on with rheostat settings initially at zero (0 milliamperes for the galvanic reading), and all cords should be checked to make sure they are not obstructed in any way. The positive electrode is attached to the client through contacts that have been treated in ways that will complete the electric circuit; this means that the metal rod or plate attached to the individual has to be coated with a special cream or gel or moistened with a low salt solution to improve conductivity. The technician should wash their own hands and the client's skin with either soap and water or a cleanser such as Savlon. The skin area is dried.

Procedures

The technician inserts the sterilized needle as previously described. The current is applied by gradually increasing the intensity on the rheostat while holding down the foot pedal (or depressing the button) until the client can feel the current, usually around 0.2 milliamps. The technician continues to hold the foot pedal down, maintaining the current, for as long as necessary to achieve the desired treatment energy (treatment energy is the product of intensity times duration). A working point

- 78 -

is established and confirmed and changes are made as needed before proceeding to other hairs.

Working point

When developing a working point on a manual galvanic electrolysis machine, the electrologist can use either a one- or two-handed method. In the one-handed technique, current is terminated by releasing the foot pedal and the needle is removed from the follicle before any attempts are made to epilate the treated hair. The initial duration of treatment is usually between 0.5 and 1 minute. If the hair glides out easily with the forceps, the working point is set, but if the hair resists loosening then other combinations of time and intensity need to be tried. In the two-handed technique, the hand not being used for the needle holder simultaneously holds a forceps to the hair with pressure during the current application. When the hair begins to come out, pressure is released from the foot pedal to terminate the current. If the bulb of the hair shaft is attached to the epilated hair, the destruction is complete and the working point is set. The technician needs to count during the procedure in order to determine the number of seconds until the hair comes out (working point duration), and thus this procedure is used less often.

Computerized features

The main features of galvanic electrolysis machines that are computerized are timers that can set the duration of each current application, the length of the treatment session, and possibly an insertion delay time. On a computerized machine with an insertion delay, there is a sensor that feels when the needle is being inserted and waits until a pre-set number of seconds before current is activated; this value should be the number of seconds until the terminus of the hair follicle is reached, about 2 to 4 seconds. The timer regulating the duration of each current application can usually be set to beep after a certain period of time from 1 to 20 seconds; the technician sets this timer to spacing and number of beeps, after which the current shuts off and the needle can be pulled out. If hairs are not easily epilated, these parameters can be reset. If the technician wishes to time the entire session, that parameter can usually be set as well.

On programmable computerized galvanic electrolysis machines, treatment energy is selected based on the type of hair. Relative treatment units for hair types ranging from vellus up to very coarse hairs are programmed into the machine with allowances for incremental changes if necessary. Many of these machines can perform more than one type of electrolysis, so the appropriate mode might need to be set (galvanic in this instance). A timer key or keys is (are) pushed to select session duration, insertion delay, thermolysis mode deactivation, and calculated duration of each electrolysis. For the latter parameter, the galvanic duration would be the selected treatment energy divided by the proposed intensity, which is generally around 0.2 milliamps or slightly higher. During the insertion, the readout or machine will distinguish between the insertion delay (no current) and the actual treatment (current activated). The machine will beep and current indicator lights will go out to indicate when to remove the needle and epilate the hair. If the hair is not easily removed, treatment energy is incrementally increased.

Programmable computerized galvanic (or multi-mode) electrolysis machines often have a hair counter, which counts the number of hairs that have been epilated during the treatment period. Another unique feature is the measurement of the galvanic after count. Basically, the galvanic after count is a repeated application of the same treatment energy in follicles when the needle has not been extracted, and it is useful when particular hairs are more distorted or coarser than others. Some degree of manual control can be maintained by the use of optional foot pedals if desired.

Multiple needle machines

Multiple needle galvanic electrolysis machines have as many as 16 different sterilized needles that are attached to different follicles and activated sequentially. Each needle is inserted and removed in sequence with the same predetermined duration and intensity and usually a 2 to 3 second insertion delay. Intensities used for this technique are relatively low, generally between 40 and 120 microamperes. The duration of insertion for each needle is 3 to 5 minutes. Epilation of the hairs after the current ceases can either be done by removing the needles and pulling each out with the tweezers or by extracting the hairs with the needles still inserted and the current continuing to flow followed by removal of the needles.

Considerations

Most of the unique considerations for performing multiple needle galvanic electrolysis center on either the need to be consistent in terms of hair type and depth or the positioning of the equipment. This technique uses a rack from which multiple needles attached to wires are taken for each insertion. This rack needs to be in close proximity to the client, and each wire attached to a needle must be just loose enough to prevent the probe from coming out or lying on the side of the follicle. A client should not move while undergoing this procedure to prevent displacement of the needles, and the possibility of dislodgement is very high for finer hair types, shallow insertion angles, and in certain areas like the chin.

Intensity and duration

In general, the intensity of treatment by a single needle galvanic apparatus is about 10 times stronger than that used for a multiple needle setup. Single needle machines usually apply about 0.1 to 1.0 milliamperes (average 0.2 to 0.5 milliamps). Multiple needle machines typically utilize intensities of about .01 to 1.0 milliamperes, but the settings are usually at the lower end of this range, in the 0.08 to .12 milliamp range. The actual treatment energy is not that different between the two techniques, however, because the time the needles remain in the follicles is longer for the multiple needle procedure. A typical single probe is inserted into a follicle for about a minute and a half (range about 15 seconds to 3 minutes), where each probe from a multiple needle apparatus applies current for about 3 to 5 minutes (range about 1 to 9 minutes).

Thermolysis by manual mode

Some machines that remove hair by thermolysis are operated manually with a foot pedal or hand-operated button. The machine is turned on with only the thermolysis mode selected (if the machine performs multiple functions) and the correct needle holder selected. Associated cords should be unobstructed. The timer control should be set to either the manual mode or the automatic timer mode if available. The rheostat that measures the intensity is initially set to zero. Pretreatment cleansing and drying of the client's skin is performed as previously described.

The actual thermolysis treatment, a high frequency alternating current which generates heat, is performed by sliding the sterilized needle into the hair follicle and then activating the current by either bearing down on the foot pedal or pushing the hand button. At the onset, the rheostat intensity is set to either zero or a very low setting, and then the intensity is gradually increased until the client feels the treatment. Current is maintained until the desired treatment energy is achieved, the foot pedal or button is released, and the hair removed with forceps by either a one- or two-handed technique.

Working point

The intensity of the current applied during thermolysis is read on a relative scale, usually from 1 to 10, with most people experiencing sensation at a reading around 2 to 4. The total treatment energy is the product of the intensity times the duration of treatment. This translates to treatment for about 5 to 10 seconds up to possibly 20 seconds for extremely coarse hairs. A working point is initially established to figure out the combination of time and intensity that easily extracts the hair without untoward side effects. This working point can be determined by either (1) applying current for a preset time period like 5 to 10 seconds, removing the probe, and then attempting to extract the hair with the forceps, or (2) applying current with the probe in one hand while grasping the hair with the forceps simultaneously in the other hand until the hair is released. In the one-handed method, reinsertion (in the same or another hair follicle) at higher treatment energy may be necessary until the hair is easily removed. For the two-handed technique, the technician needs to count during the treatment to determine seconds of time required for removal.

Alternative techniques

If the client experiences discomfort during thermolysis, the current can be delivered by pulsing or spacing it out. This is particularly useful in hypersensitive areas like the upper lip. The technician delivers the total treatment energy required by alternating intervals of current applied by the foot pedal (or button) and no current achieved by releasing the pedal. Another advantage of this technique is that the heat generated does not have time to travel back up the follicle and destroy other tissues besides the papilla. The automatic timer mode found on some of these machines is sometimes used to remove finer, relatively straight hairs by a procedure called the rapid flash technique. Here the timer is adjusted to a very short duration, usually around .05 to .1 of a second, possibly up to a second or two, and the intensity utilized is relatively high for the fine hair being extracted. This flash technique is not generally employed for coarser hairs because a large percentage of re-growth has been found to occur.

Thermolysis with a computerized machine

Typically, on a computerized machine that will perform thermolysis, that mode needs to be selected, and then a number of parameters are set on the machine. These settings include the intensity on the relative scale (usually 2 initially), the insertion delay time, the treatment duration, and if desired the beeper sound level or the total session time. The duration of each treatment is monitored by setting the number of seconds between beeps and then counting the beeps depending on the total desired length of current application. If the probe is not pulled out and the hair removed, more pulses of current will continue. There may also be a period between beeps and current application where the pulse is delayed and no energy is being transmitted, termed the pulse delay time, which can be adjusted as well.

Unique features

Most programmable computerized machines can perform electrolysis in various modes and thermolysis mode must be selected if desired. The indifferent or positive electrode, normally unnecessary for thermolysis, needs to be attached to the client. Here the electrode attachment is used as a signal to initiate current flow when the probe touches the client's skin, not as a receptacle of the flowing current. Treatment energy is initially determined by using the relative value suggested for the type of hair to be extracted and selected on the rheostat control. Other parameters are programmed into the machine including session duration and insertion delay time. Timer keys indicating the calculated duration of each thermolytic event (in other words, treatment energy/intensity) and confirmation that galvanic electrolysis is shut off are typically pressed as well. After insertion, the readout indicates whether the insertion delay or actual treatment is occurring, as well as when the current is shut off and the thermolysis complete. Most machines also have a pulsing feature that can be set. A hair counter may be included. If the apparatus includes galvanic current, it can be programmed to deliver that mode after the thermolysis.

Blend method on manually-controlled machines

Some manually-controlled foot pedal machines can perform the blend method of electrolysis. After turning the machine on and checking all cords and equipment, the positive electrode is secured to the client as previously described for the galvanic portion of the treatment. Initially both rheostats, thermolysis and galvanic electrolysis, are set to intensities of zero and the timer for the thermolysis portion is adjusted to the manual mode. The working points for both components are individually set by procedures outlined previously, starting with the thermolysis part first. The working point separately established for the galvanic removal is then divided by 3 or 4 to set a value to use in the blend method. The blend method can be performed in a variety of sequences but the most common configuration is to use galvanic electrolysis first followed by thermolysis. In this case, a single needle is inserted into the follicle, and the galvanic foot pedal is pressed and held to maintain the current. After about a second, the second thermolysis foot pedal is depressed as well and both are held for another 4 seconds. At this point, the thermolysis current is released but the galvanic is continued for another second.

Variations

The most common variation from the manual blend method is the application of intermittent bursts of thermolysis current instead of a steady unbroken flow. This is achieved by quickly depressing and letting off the thermolysis foot pedal while sustaining the galvanic current throughout. Advantages of the blend method in general include use of only about a third the amount of galvanic current and generated lye, but comparable treatment energy is maintained as a result of the heating by thermolysis. Coarse hairs are very effectively removed. Some sodium hydroxide remains in the follicle to continue destruction of the root even after epilation. There is hydrochloric acid generated by the galvanic part of the blend method, but the skin surface is sufficiently large enough to dissipate its effects.

Computerized blend method machines

On a computerized blend method machine, the equipment is set to the automatic blend mode. First the intensity, insertion delay time, and duration are selected for the galvanic electrolysis portion, and then the intensity, duration, and pulse delay timing are set for the thermolysis part. Other parameters such as beeper volume and session duration may be set as well. After pretreatment of the client's skin area, the probe selected is inserted. At this point, the machine controls all currents as indicated by lights on the machine. There are usually two different beepers as well, one signaling the start of the thermolysis portion and another indicating that the whole procedure and the galvanic current have ended. On this type of machine, the thermolysis is delivered in a series of pulses.

Procedures

For the blend method on a programmable computerized machine, the machine is initially turned on, cords and equipment are checked, and the positive electrode is attached to the client. Only the galvanic portion needs this positive electrode to complete the circuit, but here another function is to initiate current when sensors touch the skin. Total treatment energy is set based on manufacturer's recommendations for the type of hair to be epilated. The blend mode is selected, and appropriate readings for various parameters are set. A typical sequence might be to set the galvanic and then the thermolysis intensity, session time, insertion delay, and the computed timing for the thermolysis and galvanic portions. Typically, there are two needle holders on these machines so it is important to indicate which probe is being used. During the insertion, different colored lights will come on to designate what current(s) is (are) flowing, information will be displayed about the course of the treatment, and the machine should beep upon completion. Changes can be made if the treated hair is not easily epilated. A pulse feature for the thermolysis portion and a hair counter may be included options.

Intensity guidelines

In the blend method, the range of intensities utilized for the galvanic electrolysis is from about 0.1 to 1.0 milliamperes, the same as for the single modality. Since it is performed for a much shorter period of time during a blend procedure, ordinarily the actual intensity is a little higher than for galvanism alone, about 0.3 to 0.7 milliamps. Thermolysis is always set on a relative scale per manufacturer's specifications, but the range and commonly used settings resemble those used for this modality alone, generally 1 to 10 and 2 to 4 respectively. The blend method is performed in a

- 85 -

relatively short period of time, from about 5 seconds to a half minute in total. Most blend methods take about 6 to 12 seconds all together.

Kobayashi-Yamada technique

The Kobayashi-Yamada technique is a type of thermolysis technique using specially developed needles that are insulated at the top so that the pattern of damage includes approximately the bottom two-thirds of the hair follicle including the papilla. Some people believe that the more complete destruction is preferable, and there is evidence that hairs in all phases of growth can be removed with this procedure. A machine developed for this procedure can deliver more power wattage at a lower frequency (1 MHz), and all hairs in a small section are removed at one time. The biggest disadvantage of Kobayashi-Yamada is that after the procedure, the skin is generally inflamed and may not recover for several days. The only way to epilate large areas by this technique appears to be administering nerve blocks before treatment. Treatment intervals are relatively long, and many sessions are required to remove all the hair in one area. Tissue debris may be present on extracted needles necessitating frequent cleaning with alcohol swabs during the procedure.

Preparatory steps
The electrologist should familiarize themselves with the Kobayashi-Yamada manual and other updates before beginning this technique because it is controversial. It is also important to thoroughly inspect the needle to be used. Unless the needle is newly packaged and sterilized, technicians will have resterilized the needle by various means (glutaraldehyde, autoclaving, etc.) that can damage the integrity of the insulated part. Extraordinary patient preparations are generally necessary to reduce the expected inflammation and discomfort; these can be either application of local anesthesia or ice packs.

The machine is turned on and the time for each burst set with a maximum of 1 minute. The power is regulated by a foot pedal and will be shut off after current is applied for the time selected unless the manual mode is used. There may also be a control that can select intermittent bouts of current as opposed to continuous; this is called the autostepper. An intensity is set, usually in the dial range of 5 to 6 (10 to 15 watts of power). Hairs are usually counted by a display. The machine must be well ventilated so it can cool down after use. A positive pole is connected to the client in this technique. Insertions (controlled by the foot pedal) must be very accurate with the insulated part of the probe in the follicle. When the needle is removed, it may carry the epilated hair with it or use of forceps may be needed.

Needles

Design and depth of insertion
Shallow insertions have the potential to produce lesions on the skin surface regardless of modality because the density of electrons is increased in a smaller area. For galvanic electrolysis, this means that the concentration of lye is higher; for thermolysis, more heat is produced and can escape from the follicle. If the diameter of the needle is too small, theoretically more discomfort can be felt by the client in either type of procedure. The needle shape is more important for galvanic electrolysis because the entire needle is functioning as a negative electrode emitting electrons, whereas thermolysis delivers energy in a point effect primarily at the tip. Insulated probes concentrate the energy at the tip near the papilla to be destroyed and are thus useful in any electrolysis mode; their disadvantage is that repeated sterilization procedures can disrupt the integrity of the insulation.

Breakage
Detrimental effects from broken electrolysis needles stuck in hair follicles have not really been documented. Nevertheless, if this breakage occurs, the technician should attempt to extract the broken fragment by lightly kneading the area. If the needle cannot be removed, the electrologist should inform the client about the statistical improbability of any problems. Nevertheless, needles that are defective or broken or that have been reshaped after distortion should be discarded. It has been suggested that needles should be thrown out after 10 hours of usage, regardless of type. This is particularly true for smaller diameter needles. Some facilities reuse disposable needles on the same customer.

Needle holders

On electrolysis instruments, there is typically a long insulated cord that is installed into a jack. This cord is instrument specific, not interchangeable, and wires carrying the current are usually wrapped with plastic insulation. At the end of the cord, there is a rigid wider portion where the electrolysis needle is inserted. There may be more than one length of this rigid section available, generally around 3or 4 inches; shorter versions are useful for backhand insertion techniques. Newer machines generally have needle holders that the electrolysis needle can be slid into but older versions may necessitate screwing in the needle. Needle holders need to be replaced periodically several times a year. The most common problems encountered with old or defective needle holders are currents that are either too intense or sporadic. Some machines have needle holder tester incorporated into the design, or they can be sent for testing to the dealer.

Large metal surfaces

Regardless of the type of electrolysis a client is undergoing, they should not touch any large metal surfaces during the procedure. These surfaces can act as conductors of electricity. For galvanic electrolysis, current flows in a circuit from the negative electrode or cathode attached to the probe through the hair follicle and body to return through a metal plate acting as a positive electrode or anode to the power source. Touching a metal surface diverts this flow of current to that source, and thus the procedure is not as successful. In thermolysis, the current is alternating and generally vanishes into the air or through the body. Since for most of these procedures, there is no positive electrode, contact with metal completes a circuit and intensifies the amount of current and heat being generated. In the Kobayashi-Yamada variation, a positive electrode is included in order to reduce the external effects of surrounding moisture or metals.

Electrolytic effects

In addition to experimentation with different combinations of modalities, needles, times and intensities during electrolysis, there are other suggested ways to observe different electrolytic effects. Tissue destruction by either galvanism or thermolysis can be observed by substituting meat, fish, or egg whites as the protein source instead of human tissue. If a galvanic electrolysis probe is placed on a piece of meat or fish and current applied, a path of destruction can be seen along the needle. The circuit must be completed by placing the meat or fish on a metallic surface like aluminum foil and connected to the anode. If an egg white is placed in a container with similar connectors, the egg white will coagulate. Similarly, the AC of thermolysis can be applied and destruction will be observed. Here the metal surface is still required because it acts like the human body in this case. Another test is to touch a thermolysis probe to the base of a light bulb while gently increasing the intensity of the alternating current until the heat generated excites the gas inside the bulb enough to produce light.

Tissue moisture gradient

Electrical currents are conveyed more rapidly through moist tissues than dryer ones. In the region of a hair follicle, the deeper layers are moister but there is not really a gradient. Instead, the layers at and above the plane where the sebaceous gland penetrates the follicle are basically insulators that do not conduct much electricity. This is because they consist primarily of dead insoluble fibrous protein, oil and air. On the other hand, below that level, the infundibulum, the tissue is very moist and is therefore susceptible to the destructive effects of electrolysis. If the moisture sensor from a machine equipped with this type of apparatus is inserted into a follicle at different levels, the difference in conductivity between the top and bottom of the shaft can be observed. In addition, moister body areas such as the underarm serve as excellent electrical conductors.

Small concentrated section of skin

If the technician works in a small area (diameter of about 1 inch with epilated hairs about 1/8 inches apart for example), sensation in that concentrated section of skin is usually reduced. The result is less client discomfort. The downside of this system of removal is that the potential for side effects is augmented. These side effects can range from transient redness and welts to bruises or lesions. Spreading the treatments over a wider area can result in more site irritation to the client but less likelihood of undesirable side effects.

Side effects

Irritation or inflammation of the skin is generally a short-lived side effect of electrolysis; in more sensitive areas like the upper lip local swelling may occur. These discomforts can be minimized by reduction of treatment parameters, spreading out the treatment area, application of cool packs or ice or hydrocortisone cream, avoiding touching the area after the procedure, or moving the anode on the machine. The client may experience a metallic taste. Some individuals develop a short-lived condition called dermatographism in which red-edged or white wheals appear on any skin surface touched by a blunt object; this condition can be averted with use of antihistamines before treatment. If blood vessels in the area break, bruising can occur; this side effect can be reduced by pre-shaving the area to expose only growing anagen phase hair, precise insertion techniques and needle selection, or application of pressure to the bruised skin.

Blood or other tissues can seep out from the follicle because of poor technique or incorrect settings and a crust or scab can develop on the surface. This crusting usually resolves in several days. Scabbing often occurs because a needle that is too short does not penetrate into the deeper follicle regions and subsequently the treatment energy climbs back up the follicle. Other causes include current attraction to moist epidermal layers, superficial or telogen insertions, and extremely high settings. Hydrocortisone creams can aid in reducing the inflammation. Permanent skin darkening, or hyperpigmentation, in treated areas can occur in darker-skinned individuals; hydroquinone solutions may be helpful in lightening these skin areas. People with curved hair follicles can develop folliculitis if treated by thermolysis. This condition, in which the entrance to the follicle becomes inflamed, frequently occurs in individuals with current acne outbreaks or ingrown hairs as well, so those areas should not be treated. Permanent scarring or deeper tissue destruction as result of too high settings or incorrect technique are both possible but rarely observed.

Trichiasis

Trichiasis is the inward growth of hair around any body opening, a condition which generally causes irritation. The term is usually applied to inward or ingrown eyelashes that irritate the eyeball. A physician should be consulted before treating trichiasis by electrolysis. There are local anesthetics available by prescription that can be used in the eye area to numb it before the procedure. To remove these hairs, the Electrologist needs to firmly grasp the eyelid with their free hand and draw it away from the eyeball. Though delicate, this procedure can be accomplished by a skillful technician, and in fact the electrolysis technique was first used in this eyelash area.

Bead sterilizer

A bead sterilizer is an apparatus that destroys microorganisms by heating glass beads in a well to very high temperatures (about 480 to 500 degrees Fahrenheit) and then placing equipment to be sterilized amongst the beads for short periods of time (a minute or less). The longer sterilization times are appropriate for needles that are not client-specific. Theoretically hepatitis B and HIV viruses, the greatest concerns, should be destroyed under these conditions. This sterilization technique was widely used at one time, but it is no longer generally recommended or endorsed by recognized authorities. Therefore, its description is included for informational purposes only.

Purchasing an electrolysis machine

In many localities, electrolysis machines can only be purchased by either trained electrologists or licensed physicians. Machines bought for use in the United States and Canada must adhere to frequency regulations established by the Federal Communications Commission (FCC) or the Canadian Standards Association (CSA) respectively; both permit only 13.56 megahertz or 2 and 3 multiples of this frequency. Voltage capability in these countries must be within 10 volts of the common 110 volts. Cost, service, type, functions available, and additional features are all important considerations. Machines that perform only thermolysis will be ineffective for many types of follicles. Instruments that can perform multiple functions incorporating thermolysis, galvanic electrolysis or multiple needle galvanism, and especially the blend method are preferable. Computerized instruments and the programmable machines are more expensive, but may be worth the cost in terms of ease of use and improved technique. The availability of pulsing modes, hair counters, various timers, and other available features may influence machine selection.

Positive electrodes

The positive electrode is also known as the indifferent electrode. On most instruments, it is attached to an insulated cable that is inserted into the machine's anode. The other end is connected to the client via some sort of metal rod or plate to complete the circuit (except with some strictly thermolysis machines). The ability to conduct this current back to the machine is augmented at the positive electrode by use of special creams, gels, and/or pads soaked in weak salt solutions in contact with the client. Again this electrode can fail for reasons similar to the needle holder, and it should be periodically checked and changed. These electrodes should also be washed and dried off at the end of a session to prevent rusting.

Pore markers

There are creams available that have dyes or other coloring agents incorporating into them. These are called pore markers or sometimes follicle enhancers. They are sometimes used to identify or draw attention to the follicle aperture when epilating delicate, light-colored blond hairs. The cream is spread over the area and the surplus is removed with a suitable cleanser such as Savlon. Pore markers are unnecessary for most types of hairs and areas.

Percentage of hairs

The percentage of hairs in the resting telogen phase differs according to the area of the body. New anagen phase hairs will eventually re-grow out of these follicles. If other non-permanent hair removal techniques have been previously used, the percentage of telogen hairs can be as high as 80% on the leg for example. This means only 20% of these leg hairs are permanently removed each session, so the client needs to come at least 5 times and possibly more because re-growth can be up to 50% even with good technique. In addition, new follicles may be stimulated; this is especially true for menopausal women who may be producing hormones.

Duration per session

The actual electrolysis time needed for smaller areas such as the chin of a menopausal woman or the moustache region is relatively short, about 15 minutes to a half hour. Multiple sessions are required, however, generally about 6 visits over several months for the chin and weekly for about a half year tapering to longer intervals for up to a total of 2 years for the moustache area. Females with large amounts of unwanted facial hair may need to up to 3 hours a week initially for a year and about an hour a week over the next year. Removal of hair in the armpits generally necessitates about 10 hours of removal time spread over 5 to 10 sessions. The arms, legs, back and breast areas all have high percentages of resting phase hairs and require multiple treatments. For the arms, legs, and back, pre-shaving is helpful in exposing more of the anagen phase hairs that can potentially be permanently removed

Speed of removal

Hair removal using the galvanic electrolysis modality alone is the slowest technique. The fastest removal can be accomplished in about 15 seconds but coarse hairs can take up to 3 minutes each; speed can be improved with the multiple needle variation. On the other hand, anywhere from about 150 to 320 hairs can be epilated in an hour with thermolysis alone or the blend method. The flash technique can be used for finer hair types to improve the speed, but it is not particularly efficacious for coarser or wavy hairs or with distorted follicles resulting in high rates of re-growth.

Laser and Light-Based Epilators

Lasers

Lasers are concentrated beams of monochromatic (one wavelength) light. They are produced by the excitation of gases or minerals by an electrical current. Their theoretical effectiveness in hair reduction, not permanent removal, is based on the tenet of selective photothermolysis, which proposes that specific wavelengths of light target specific tissues. Thus lasers selected for hair reduction techniques are in the wavelength range that can target the melanin in hairs in the vicinity of the dermal papilla without destroying other vital cells like red blood cells or the dermis. This wavelength range is about 700 to 1000 nm. Small amounts of energy are also absorbed by the oxyhemoglobin protein in red blood cells and water at these wavelengths. Only darker hairs have significant amounts of melanin and so they are most effectively reduced. The pigment absorbs the light and is heated, and the papilla is damaged and vaporizes.

Laser sources

The most common laser sources for hair reduction are either the ruby rod, which emits light at wavelength of 694 nm, and the Nd:YAG combination, whose wavelength is 1064 nm. Nd refers to the element neodymium and YAG is the abbreviation for the synthetic gemstone comprised of yttrium, aluminum, and garnet. These are both at the ends of the effective 700 to 1000 nm range. Other sources are inappropriate because they emit lasers than can destroy other tissues in the area of the papilla. For example, the short wavelengths produced from argon gas, 488 or 514.5 nm, can destroy red blood cells. Lasers elicited from carbon dioxide have wide-ranging, not selective, destructive effects and are more useful for destroying the entire epidermal layer.

Types of lasers

The Food and Drug Administration (FDA) has approved 4 types of lasers for hair reduction, but not permanent hair removal. The NeoDymium Yttrium Aluminum Garnets (Nd:YAGs) devices have the longest pulse or wavelength, 1064 nm. These devices are also the most effective, they produce the fewest side effects, and they elicit less discomfort than some other laser types. Ruby, alexandrite, and diode lasers emit shorter wavelengths, 694, 755, and 810 nm respectively. All three have been approved by the FDA, but their effectiveness remains debatable. The ruby lasers may not probe deeply enough into the hair follicle to destroy much of the dermal papilla. The other two versions have not been well studied and may produce unwanted side effects. For example, diode lasers appear to elicit superficial hive-like reactions.

Apparatus that produces a laser

An apparatus that produces a laser typically consists of an energy source that uses a process called pumping to bombard or excite another material, called the active medium. For lasers used in hair reduction, the energy source is electricity and the active mediums are the elements that absorb and accumulate the energy. The most common active mediums are Nd:YAG or a ruby rod. The third part of the laser apparatus is the compartment that surrounds the active medium, called either the optical cavity or resonator.

The electrical bombardment from the energy source raises some of the atoms of the active material from their lowest energy ground state to higher energy levels termed excited states. These excited states consist of very high energy singlet states initially achieved and possible subsequent intermediate energy levels called metastable. A proportion of the atoms achieve this relatively balanced metastable state, and as they eventually go back to the ground state, they give off electromagnetic radiation or photons of light. For the duration of exposure to the energy source, photons emitted collide with other metastable atoms stimulating them to emit light at equivalent energy levels and wavelengths. In addition, all these photons are in phase with each other. The optical cavity uses mirrors to intensify and reflect this photon cascade and direct the laser beam.

Parameters

Laser equipment for hair reduction has a number of either inherent or controllable parameters that can determine its effectiveness and limit other damage. The choice of active medium determines the wavelength of emission and chromophore targeted. Wavelength is expressed in nanometers (nm); 1 nm equals one billionth of a meter. The amount of work or energy fluence is measure in joules/cm^2, and is related to the width of laser beam. The thermal storage coefficient (abbreviated Tr_2) quantifies the maximum amount of heat that can be retained by a particular type of hair before damage will be deflected to other tissues.

Laser pulse duration

The time the laser light is directed to the target (the hair follicle in hair reduction) is called the pulse duration or width. This duration is very short, measured in milliseconds (ms), but can vary according to active medium used and specific equipment. The basic tenet is that the length of time the laser energy is applied should match the work or energy flounce necessary for removal. This means coarser hairs theoretically require longer pulse durations. In addition, the pulse duration has to be set in a range that will retain the heat in the hair follicle without dissipating it to surrounding tissue. Here the concept of thermal relaxation time (TRT), the period it takes before half of the heat energy moves elsewhere, is important. The TRT of the hair follicle is longer than that of the epidermis, so the ideal pulse duration is somewhere in between the two times.

Laser spot size

The width of the generated laser beam is termed the spot size, typically measured for hair reduction techniques in millimeters (mm). Wider beams necessitate more work or fluence in order to be effective. In addition, spot size is larger at the skin surface than in deeper layers because the tissues scatter some of the light; this phenomenon is called dermal scattering. In order to access the target, presumably the dermal papilla region, the relationship of spot size to desired depth should be about 4:1, with a typical spot size of 7 to 10 mm.

Laser beams can be used at higher levels of work or fluence if the skin is cooled to avert epidermal tissue destruction. This is particularly useful for darker skin types that may have pigmentation in the skin that absorbs some of the light energy. There are various cooling techniques. Some utilize applied sources of cold, such as cooled gels that are put on the skin or cryogenic sprays that produce very low temperatures. Other cold devices are incorporated into the laser equipment, such as cold circulating water pumps or handpieces that have tips that can be cooled.

Laser handpieces

Laser handpieces come in a variety of shapes and the resultant laser beams are emitted in the same pattern. For effective treatment, the light must cover the entire area targeted. If the beams are directed in any type of shape with squared-off corners, whether hexagonal, square, or rectangular, they can fit together by abutting against each other. If, on the other hand, round handpieces are utilized, the beams are also rounded and thus the composite either misses areas or results in overlaps. In the latter case, the overlapped areas can receive too much treatment. Lasers that use some type of mechanical device to separate light emitted into very fast but intense pulses are called pulse lasers. These types of lasers are usually used to remove dark lesions or tattoos.

Laser hair removal devices availability

A number of laser hair removal devices utilize Nd:YAG, wavelength 1064 nm, as the active medium. Several use relatively long pulse durations of up to 100 milliseconds, spot sizes in ranges from 2 to 9 millimeters, and features such as scanners and cooling devices. Nd:YAG laser machines that emit very rapid bursts of pulses, a technique called Q-Switching, are also available. A number of ruby laser apparatuses, wavelength 694 nm, are sold that have very short pulse durations (up to about 3 msec) and spot sizes in the range of about 6 to 12 mm; they generally incorporate cooling devices and may offer other modes. The current alexandrite laser devices emit light at a 755 nm wavelength, pulse in a range of 3 up to 40 milliseconds, have spot sizes varying from 5 up to 18 mm, and may again have cooling handpieces or scanners. There are also diode devices available that emit light at 800 nm, can be used at longer pulse times of up to 250 msec depending on the device, and use mid-range spot sizes. Intense pulsed light is the mode on at least one device.

Ethnic groups

Laser hair removal is most effective in individuals of Eastern Asian descent because they have dark hairs targeted by the laser yet very little pigmentation in their skin to absorb the energy. Similarly people of Middle Eastern or Mediterranean background may be good candidates. These individuals tend to have greater amounts of hair in the facial and bodily areas, but many also have relatively light skins. In addition, they can use bleaches like 4% hydroquinone to reduce skin pigmentation. The effectiveness of laser hair removal in those

- 97 -

of Caucasian European descent is highly variable depending on the combination of hair and skin pigmentation. Anyone of African background is generally not recommended for laser hair removal techniques because their highly pigmented skin diverts the laser beam away from the dermal papilla and can result in burning and scarring.

Laser light vs. traditional light

Traditional light is a continuum of wavelengths in the visible range. These numerous wavelengths can be visible as many different colors and thus traditional light is said to be polychromatic. Traditional light scatters in many directions, losing its intensity with distance from the source. On the other hand, laser light is very intense and unidirectional, or collimated. The waves of light produced by the laser apparatus all run in phase, in parallel, and in the same direction and are said to be coherent. Lastly, laser light consists of only one wavelength and thus only a single color or type of pigment can absorb this light. Thus lasers are monochromatic instead of polychromatic.

Photoepilation

Photoepilation is hair removal by a light source that has been filtered for selectivity. This technique is often alternatively referred to as intense pulse light (IPL) or by other names. A white light source covering the visible and near or low range infrared spectrum, from about 400 to 1200 nm in multiple wavelengths, is used. The technician activates filters that remove certain lower wavelengths that are unwanted leaving those that target the desired tissues. The light is pulsed up to 4 times for very brief time periods, with an average of about 35 milliseconds (.035 seconds). The level of energy, however, approximates that of laser beam in terms of energy per unit area, or joules/cm^2. The light undergoes a variety of changes before being absorbed and this procedure is generally felt to be safer than laser techniques.

Grothus Draper Law

The Grothus Draper law is a principle that expounds that absorption of light must occur in biological tissue before any damage or other effects can take place. This is extremely applicable to the use of lasers because they emit a single wavelength and target only tissues that can selectively absorb that particular wavelength. Actually what is being targeted is the group of atoms in the biological tissue that absorbs this wavelength; this collection of atoms is called the chromophore. For hair reduction techniques, the chromophore is melanin which attracts the photons and changes them into thermal energy in the form of heat which facilitates hair destruction.

Fitzpatrick Skin Phototype scale

The Fitzpatrick Skin Phototype scale defines 6 skin types; it relates the skin pigmentation levels combined with hair and eye color to the tendency of that skin type to tan or burn. The fairest individuals also have blond or pale red hair and blue or green eyes and are termed Type 1; these people cannot tan and will burn. Fair people with light brown or red hair and green or brown eyes tend to burn as well but may tan and are classified as Type 2. Individuals with a little more pigmentation with brown hair and eyes are termed Type 3 and they frequently tan but can burn. The last three types never tend to normally sunburn but have higher levels of skin pigmentation that can be detrimental during laser procedures. Type IV is characterized by olive skin and brown or black hair and eyes. Individuals that are either Type V or VI have black hair and eyes; the difference is their skin color (dark brown versus black).

Lancer Ethnicity Scale

The Lancer Ethnicity Scale is a little more simplistic than the Fitzpatrick typing. The Lancer scale relates skin pigmentation levels and ethnic origin and translates those into 6 skin types. The first three types, Skin Type I, II and III, encompass varying degrees of so-called "white" skin colors ranging from light to dark white and correspond to the same classifications as the Fitzpatrick Skin Phototype scale. The other classifications on the Lancer Ethnicity Scale relate ethnic origin to intensities of "brown" skin color. Here the relationship to the Fitzpatrick classifications becomes fuzzier, because an individual who is Skin Type IV, V or VI on the Lancer Ethnicity Scale could fall into any of the latter three skin types defined by the Fitzpatrick scale.

Current regulatory agencies

Laser hair removal devices must be approved by the Food and Drug Administration (FDA) and its subsidiary branch called the Center for Devices and Radiological Health (CDRH). Another federal agency, the Occupational Safety and Health Administration (OSHA), normally governs employee safety issues. OSHA has currently adopted the guidelines set forth by the nonprofit group called the American National Standards Institute (ANSI)for facilities performing laser techniques. There is also a professional group called the Society for Clinical and Medical Hair Removal, Inc. (SCMHR) that is active in evaluating laser and other hair removal techniques.

Laser hair reduction techniques

One of the most important aspects of setting up a laser hair reduction facility is the ability to have a special room that bars entrance during procedures, blocks out other light, and has no reflective surfaces. Protective eyewear that has been sanctioned by the ANSI must always be worn by both the technician and the client to avoid possible laser-induced blindness. The laser equipment must be individually grounded, ventilated, kept in good shape, regularly calibrated, and routinely cleansed to remove carbon accumulation. Everyone in the room must remove all jewelry or reflective clothing. The trained laser removal specialist must thoroughly inform the customer about the process and perform a patch test before proceeding with the laser or intense pulsed light procedure. The facility must have insurance procedures set up prior to practicing laser or IPL techniques.

Advantages and disadvantages

Laser hair removal is a relatively fast technique compared to electrolysis because more than one hair can be targeted at a time. Since the skin is not pierced by any equipment, there is no possibility of blood-borne disease transmission. Hair removal lasts a long time, sometimes permanently, and re-growth can be fine and light colored which may be preferable. The comfort level compared to electrolysis is debatable. On the other hand, true permanent removal may not be achieved. Laser techniques are expensive and usually require multiple appointments. Protective eyewear is essential during the treatment period. Only certain skin types can expect good results; light or non-pigmented hairs do not absorb the light emitted whereas darker skin will divert it. At present, the safety of these procedures is still not well documented or controlled.

Contraindications

In general, laser hair removal can be performed anywhere except below the eyebrow and in the ear area. The expected effectiveness of the technique is related to skin type and hair color. There are quite a few situations that preclude laser hair removal, however. Some of these conditions are similar to the contraindications for electrolysis (such as diabetes, epilepsy or presence of skin lesions), but there are laser-specific ones as well. If a person is taking any medication that increases their sensitivity to electromagnetic radiation, they should not undergo laser treatments; these photosensitizing drugs include tetracycline and Retin-A. If the individual is predisposed to keloid scarring, lasers should not be used. Laser removal will be ineffective for gray hairs or with the inherited condition called albinism where hair and skin pigmentation are lacking. These techniques should be avoided during episodes of sunburn and in unclassified cases of hirsutism.

Pre-laser removal

A client desiring laser hair reduction techniques must terminate use of any medication that can cause photosensitivity several months before beginning treatments. These pre-treatment periods of drug removal range from 3 months for Accutane to 6 months for tetracyclines or Retin-A. The individual must also stop all other hair removal modalities for a minimum of 10 weeks prior to laser treatments except for shaving and depilatory use. The purpose is to have the maximum percentage of growing hairs available to be targeted. The client should have had a consultation with the laser specialist and filled out appropriate records including medical and hair removal history as well as skin type and markings.

The client may have applied a topical anesthetic to reduce pain shortly before the treatment. In the treatment room in privacy, they don a gown and other draping if needed. Photos of the area to be treated are taken if this has not been down previously. The skin area to be treated is cleansed, shaved, and cooled. The client and technician both need to put on safety goggles at this point. The laser apparatus is normally locked up so it needs to be unchained and settings programmed according to recommendations for hair and skin type.

Patch test

In the context of laser hair removal, a patch test is a pre-treatment check of the fluence or energy concentration that the client can tolerate. A spot close to the intended treatment section is pulsed one time. Then the epidermal layer is inspected for the presence of the Nikolski sign, which is either blistering or severance of the epidermal layer. If such signs are present, then the fluence is reduced by about 5 to 10 joules per square centimeter until the energy level that will not produce these untoward effects is found. Use of the patch test also familiarizes the client with the procedure.

The greatest fluence of laser energy that the client can stand without untoward effects is used. This fluence is predetermined by the patch test usually. The handpiece is tightly pressed against the skin to diffuse the absorptive chromophore oxyhemoglobin away from the laser path and shorten the distance to the papilla. Pulse times or fluence can be changed during the session if the individual experiences discomfort. The laser treatment turns the hairs into carbon particles which accumulate on the window of the apparatus and need to be periodically wiped off with alcohol. Treatment sessions can range from 10 minutes for the facial area up to an hour for removal for an entire leg. At the completion of the session, the equipment is turned off and locked. The handpiece must be disinfected between treatments.

Post-laser hair treatment

Often there is a transient redness and swelling in the area after laser hair removal techniques, especially with shorter wavelength lasers. Surface blistering or crusting may occur as well. Small bumps and other swelling can occur temporarily with longer wavelength treatments. The skin in the area may be too highly or hyperpigmented, a condition that can be reduced by bleaching with hydroquinone, but in rare instances permanent decreases in skin coloration can occur. Within several days, small black spots of burnt hair will become visible at treated follicles but they will eventually be ejected from the follicle; this phenomenon is termed splattering. New hairs will appear at various time intervals afterwards in areas where hairs were either missed or not actively growing or where new follicles have been stimulated.

After having laser hair removal treatments, the client is prone to discomfort and other reactions that must be alleviated. Burning usually needs to be assuaged by application of cold, either aloe vera or other topical preparations, cold packs, or a bag or glove of ice. Total sunblocks with high SPFs generally need to be put on the treated area to block ultraviolet light. Brand new makeup can be put on areas that are intact, and this will also provide further UV protection. Another session should be scheduled in 6 weeks to 2 months.

Home care
The immediate recommendations for the client who has received laser treatments center on alleviation of the burning and blistering side effects of the procedure. At home, the individual should periodically apply clean cold packs, calming ointments, and if blistering occurs antibiotic preparations to the treated area. Hot baths are contraindicated for at least a day; instead they should take short, tepid showers. The client should be told to stay away from the sun for 3 weeks or until their next session. A sunscreen with a sun protection factor of at least 15 should be used if they experience any redness. Makeup can be used in intact skin areas but it must be new and applied as antiseptically as possible.

- 103 -

Business Practices

Business plan

A business plan is a document that specifies all features of a business as it exists or as it is envisioned. Usually a business plan includes a primary listing of all pertinent business aspects and a secondary listing of anything relevant to the primary components of the plan. Some of these features apply to most businesses such as name, location and type of facility, type of ownership, required licenses, zoning regulations and permit, method of funding, insurance, advertising, and expansion plans if relevant. For a business offering electrolysis, more specific parts of the business plan might include the range of hair removal procedures included, local demand for these services, and the customer base. New businesses may present this business plan to any possible affiliates such as financiers, lawyers, or real estate professionals. The plan should be carefully organized into a binder or other format.

Business ownership

When there is a single individual who owns and operates a business, the type of ownership is called a sole proprietorship. A variant of this type of ownership in which the name of the business is different from the individual's legal name is termed DBA (doing business as), and here a permit is necessary. When a business is jointly owned by two or more individuals, it is termed a partnership. This type of arrangement necessitates the use of a legal contract that spells out the terms of the partnership and the proportion of legal liability in matters related to the business. A business is said to be incorporated, or defined as a corporation, if it is identified as such and adopts a charter that adheres to state regulations and taxation policies. Usually there are directors, shareholders and multiple employees in a corporation setup, but a single owner can incorporate their business as well to avoid claims against their personal wealth. Larger corporations issue publicly-traded shares of stock representing the value of the business.

Financing

A new business plan should detail how capital to finance the business will be raised. Capital refers to the amount of money needed, and it consists of available cash plus venture financing that needs to be acquired. Venture capital can come from either private investment or from loans to be repaid in the future. In general, loan requests to banks or other institutions should include a cushion amount to cover unexpected expenses. New businesses often take about a year to become recognized and profitable. Financial institutions usually require information about facility type, location, size, and leasing terms before they will issue a business loan.

Laws and regulations

Businesses must adhere to laws and regulations at the local, state, and federal level. Therefore, a prospective business owner must acquaint themselves with all of these. Local bodies may regulate issues such as building codes and parking. Typically, state laws specify sales tax rates, licensing requirements, and methods of dealing with payroll taxes and other compensation. On a federal level, the laws primarily cover either the distribution of taxes and insurance as well as safety requirements dictated by OSHA. Federal taxes include payroll, unemployment, and Social Security taxes.

Setup and location

The location of any business contributes to its potential for success in terms of attracting clients. Some locations can provide a built-in customer base or visibility to bring new clients in. If the facility is inviting and provides amenities like parking or proximity to public transportation, more clients can be drawn in. The setup of the facility itself is important. It should be large enough to have an attractive reception area, office, as many treatment rooms as needed, restrooms, storage areas, and possibly laundry capabilities. All business should be handicapped accessible, well-lit, and well-ventilated. If there is more than one floor, there must be an elevator. Accommodation for future growth of the business is another consideration.

Lease

A lease is a legally-binding agreement between two parties in which real estate and equipment is rented for a specified amount of money and period of time. The business owner or entrepreneur renting the space should employ a lawyer to examine the terms of the lease before signing it. The responsibility for variables like plumbing and electrical installation should be identified in the lease. The length of the lease and the monthly or other fee for the lessee should be clearly stated. A building inspection should be done and certificate of occupancy permit issued before moving in, especially if the building is new construction.

Home-based vs. existing business

A home-based business requires little overhead and no travel time, and it can be tax deductible. However, this type of business is difficult to advertise and provide access to. It requires a residential zoning permit that is typically issued by some local governing body such as the town hall. The potential business owner may need to present their plans for approval by the community, including things like how they plan to address flow of clients, parking, and such. Appropriate licensures and certificates at the local, state, and federal still need to be obtained; these include federal and state tax identification numbers. Sometimes an existing business can be bought; here both a lawyer and an accountant should be consulted before purchase.

An electrologist can establish their own business facility, work out of their home within legal limitations, or join a larger electrolysis studio or chain. There are also other types of businesses that might employ or associate themselves with electrologists. These include certain doctor's offices or medical clinics, hospitals, health clubs, hairstyling or other cosmetic businesses, and sometimes department stores. In these instances, the electrologist may be an employee instead of an independent operator, and wages may be relatively low in these types of facilities.

Insurance

There are three types of insurance that a hair removal business should purchase, preferably from a single company. The first is malpractice insurance, which covers potential negligence by the professionals employed at the facility. These policies should clearly state which professionals and equipment are covered. Incorporation provides personal protection in the event of a lawsuit. Policies for business owner's liability insurance can offer a variety of coverage such as theft, water damage, security breaches, and various natural disasters. Anyone performing hair removal should also be covered by personal disability insurance that pays an individual who becomes disabled and cannot work.

Overhead

Overhead is the general underlying cost of running a business. This cost is naturally lower for a home-based business because one of the major overhead costs, facility rental or leasing, is eliminated. Nevertheless, any type of hair removal business will have the other overhead expenditures of equipment leasing or purchase, products and supplies associated with the processes offered, marketing and advertisements, and salaries to employees if applicable. There are other expenses associated with the cleaning of the facility and non-disposable equipment, as well as water and gas or electricity costs. All of these overhead costs need to be considered when establishing charges for services.

Tax considerations

A federal tax identification number is required to operate a business with employees. In addition, a state sales tax identification number is usually required if products or other taxable services are offered; the business owner must be familiar with and comply with their state regulations. It is preferable to have a dedicated business bank account. Bookkeeping is essential, and hiring a certified public accountant (CPA) to provide tax-related expertise is recommended. Mechanisms to settle the day's receipts and close the facility daily should be clearly identified, especially if there are employees in the business. Depending on the scope of the business, payroll issues can be covered by either computer software or professionals such as the accountant or other companies that disperse wages. In addition, the owner should find out whether medically-prescribed electrolysis treatments are tax deductible in their jurisdiction or covered by insurance, and inform clients about these possibilities.

Employees

Ideally, hiring an employee begins with a review of their qualifications and then a personal interview. During the interview, the prospective employer should appraise the candidate's application, background and experience, legal work status, and applicable certificates or licenses. The employer has some responsibilities during the interview process as well. They should clearly identify the scope of the position, compensation, benefits if available, and hours to be worked. The owner should show the candidate the entire facility and discuss other personnel policies with the candidate. It is advisable to have an employee manual available to clarify any possible issues. The prospective employee should be hired or rejected in a timely manner; if hired they need to complete federal and other hiring forms as soon as possible. Yearly evaluation forms are suggested for individuals hired. If termination becomes necessary, reasons should be clearly stated and the action performed promptly and professionally.

Advertising

Today a website on the World Wide Web is a cheap and very useful way to advertise a business. More traditional methods of advertising such as business cards, brochures, mass mailings, coupons, and print ads in newspapers, event programs, or the yellow pages are relatively inexpensive means of advertising as well. Television and radio spots are more expensive, but depending on the scope of the business they may be cost-effective. Establishing good relationships with clients is one of the best ways to advertise a business because hopefully they will refer the business to other possible customers. A business that has maintained a quality operation for a minimum of 5 years may be invited to join the Better Business Bureau (BBB); membership in the BBB can be a great advertising tool as well.

Record keeping

Home-based or smaller electrolysis or hair removal facilities should maintain an electrolysis client chart for each customer. This client chart should include name, contact information (unless kept elsewhere), treatment date, skin condition at the site of electrolysis or other removal, area of removal and consistency of hairs, length of treatment, modality employed, treatment parameters, and probe size. Subsequent sessions may be recorded on the same chart. An appointment (and possibly day) book or computer scheduling capabilities are necessary, including the ability to show changes easily. The client list with contact information is extremely important; it should be kept in a secure place and can be sold often if the business is transferred. Forms for periodic quality control should be available.

Bookkeeping and tax-related practices should be defined and maintained; a bookkeeper and accountant may be retained for these purposes. Larger practices, particularly those involving other employees, may require additional record keeping.

Professionalism and ethics

It is important for an Electrologist or anyone else in the workplace to maintain an attitude of professionalism in or outside the confines of the work facility. Professionalism refers to the skill, proficiency, and attitude of members of a trained profession such as electrolysis. Components of professionalism include promptness; proper dress (including non-revealing clothing and laundered lab coats); avoidance of vulgar, offensive, or other inappropriate language; conducting the treatment in a non-threatening manner (for example, use of draping); and maintaining the highest possible demeanor in or outside the workplace. Professionalism also means either practicing or at least being aware of the latest treatment options. Ethics refers to a code of moral principles, and the Electrologist should strive to maintain professional ethics.

Licensing requirements

As of February 2006, 34 of 50 of the United States had some sort of licensing requirement for the practice of electrology. Fifteen states regulated the industry under a State Board of Cosmetology or something similar. Many other states used the Department of Public Health or some type of medical board. The durations of regulated electrology curriculums were as little as 125 hours and as long as 450 hours or even more, and some courses are as short as 60 hours part-time or as long as full-time for 2 years or other variations. Generally, a high school diploma or equivalency and/or a minimum age of 18 years were required for the licensed practice of electrology. In some instances, an apprenticeship can be used in lieu of formal training. Requirements in foreign countries run the gamut from no formal licensing requirements to use only by practicing physicians.

Licensing requirements for electrologists vary greatly by state and country. There are, however, several professional organizations that one can join. Each focuses on aspects of professionalism, education, business promotion, legal issues, insurance, or further certification. One of the leading organizations is the American Electrology Association, www.electrology.com; this group emphasizes legal aspects, licensure, quality standards, and public consciousness and offers the Certified Professional Electrologist (CPE). A similar organization is the International Guild of Professional Electrologists, Inc., www.igpe.org; the major difference between the two groups is that the latter advocates incorporation of laser and other new methodologies into the practice of electrology. The Society for Clinical and Medical Hair Removal, Inc., www.scmhr.org, also supports the addition of light-based techniques and offers two types of certification, the Certified Clinical Electrologist (CCE) and a higher designation, the Clinical Medical Electrologist (CME).

Continuing education credits

Continuing education credits (CEUs) or something similar is available in many different professional fields. CEUs are credits issued by recognized national organizations after completion of classes or conferences pertaining to an individual's field of endeavor. For electrologists, membership in professional organizations may be contingent on regular completion of continuing education credits. Ways of obtaining CEUs include conference attendance, online classes, and mail-order courses.

Conferences

One of the best ways to keep abreast of the latest information is to attend conferences related to electrology. There are also a number of publications related to electrology. Most of these are journals published at various intervals. These journals include the Journal of Electrology, International Hair Route, Electrolysis World, and Electrologist's Digest. In addition, equipment manufacturers and other companies provide periodic updates and other information on equipment and techniques. For example, the United Professional Electrolysis Manufacturers Association (UPEMA) sponsors informative trade shows and educational materials, and the Instantron Company also publishes reports about equipment and techniques. Government bodies such as the Food and Drug Administration in the United States can provide information as well. Information about early research and the scientific basis of techniques can be found in medical libraries.

Secret Key #1 - Time is Your Greatest Enemy

Pace Yourself

Wear a watch. At the beginning of the test, check the time (or start a chronometer on your watch to count the minutes), and check the time after every few questions to make sure you are "on schedule."

If you are forced to speed up, do it efficiently. Usually one or more answer choices can be eliminated without too much difficulty. Above all, don't panic. Don't speed up and just begin guessing at random choices. By pacing yourself, and continually monitoring your progress against your watch, you will always know exactly how far ahead or behind you are with your available time. If you find that you are one minute behind on the test, don't skip one question without spending any time on it, just to catch back up. Take 15 fewer seconds on the next four questions, and after four questions you'll have caught back up. Once you catch back up, you can continue working each problem at your normal pace.

Furthermore, don't dwell on the problems that you were rushed on. If a problem was taking up too much time and you made a hurried guess, it must be difficult. The difficult questions are the ones you are most likely to miss anyway, so it isn't a big loss. It is better to end with more time than you need than to run out of time.

Lastly, sometimes it is beneficial to slow down if you are constantly getting ahead of time. You are always more likely to catch a careless mistake by working more slowly than quickly, and among very high-scoring test takers (those who are likely to have lots of time left over), careless errors affect the score more than mastery of material.

Secret Key #2 - Guessing is not Guesswork

You probably know that guessing is a good idea - unlike other standardized tests, there is no penalty for getting a wrong answer. Even if you have no idea about a question, you still have a 20-25% chance of getting it right.

Most test takers do not understand the impact that proper guessing can have on their score. Unless you score extremely high, guessing will significantly contribute to your final score.

Monkeys Take the Test

What most test takers don't realize is that to insure that 20-25% chance, you have to guess randomly. If you put 20 monkeys in a room to take this test, assuming they answered once per question and behaved themselves, on average they would get 20-25% of the questions correct. Put 20 test takers in the room, and the average will be much lower among guessed questions. Why?

1. The test writers intentionally writes deceptive answer choices that "look" right. A test taker has no idea about a question, so picks the "best looking" answer, which is often wrong. The monkey has no idea what looks good and what doesn't, so will consistently be lucky about 20-25% of the time.

2. Test takers will eliminate answer choices from the guessing pool based on a hunch or intuition. Simple but correct answers often get excluded, leaving a 0% chance of being correct. The monkey has no clue, and often gets lucky with the best choice.

This is why the process of elimination endorsed by most test courses is flawed and detrimental to your performance- test takers don't guess, they make an ignorant stab in the dark that is usually worse than random.

$5 Challenge

Let me introduce one of the most valuable ideas of this course- the $5 challenge:

- 112 -

You only mark your "best guess" if you are willing to bet $5 on it.

You only eliminate choices from guessing if you are willing to bet $5 on it.

Why $5? Five dollars is an amount of money that is small yet not insignificant, and can really add up fast (20 questions could cost you $100). Likewise, each answer choice on one question of the test will have a small impact on your overall score, but it can really add up to a lot of points in the end.

The process of elimination IS valuable. The following shows your chance of guessing it right:

If you eliminate wrong answer choices until only this many remain:	1	2	3
Chance of getting it correct:	100%	50%	33%

However, if you accidentally eliminate the right answer or go on a hunch for an incorrect answer, your chances drop dramatically: to 0%. By guessing among all the answer choices, you are GUARANTEED to have a shot at the right answer.

That's why the $5 test is so valuable- if you give up the advantage and safety of a pure guess, it had better be worth the risk.

What we still haven't covered is how to be sure that whatever guess you make is truly random. Here's the easiest way:

Always pick the first answer choice among those remaining.

Such a technique means that you have decided, **before you see a single test question**, exactly how you are going to guess- and since the order of choices tells you nothing about which one is correct, this guessing technique is perfectly random.

- 113 -

This section is not meant to scare you away from making educated guesses or eliminating choices- you just need to define when a choice is worth eliminating. The $5 test, along with a pre-defined random guessing strategy, is the best way to make sure you reap all of the benefits of guessing.

Secret Key #3 - Practice Smarter, Not Harder

Many test takers delay the test preparation process because they dread the awful amounts of practice time they think necessary to succeed on the test. We have refined an effective method that will take you only a fraction of the time.

There are a number of "obstacles" in your way to succeed. Among these are answering questions, finishing in time, and mastering test-taking strategies. All must be executed on the day of the test at peak performance, or your score will suffer. The test is a mental marathon that has a large impact on your future.

Just like a marathon runner, it is important to work your way up to the full challenge. So first you just worry about questions, and then time, and finally strategy:

Success Strategy

1. Find a good source for practice tests.
2. If you are willing to make a larger time investment, consider using more than one study guide- often the different approaches of multiple authors will help you "get" difficult concepts.
3. Take a practice test with no time constraints, with all study helps "open book." Take your time with questions and focus on applying strategies.
4. Take a practice test with time constraints, with all guides "open book."
5. Take a final practice test with no open material and time limits

If you have time to take more practice tests, just repeat step 5. By gradually exposing yourself to the full rigors of the test environment, you will condition your mind to the stress of test day and maximize your success.

Secret Key #4 - Prepare, Don't Procrastinate

Let me state an obvious fact: if you take the test three times, you will get three different scores. This is due to the way you feel on test day, the level of preparedness you have, and, despite the test writers' claims to the contrary, some tests WILL be easier for you than others.

Since your future depends so much on your score, you should maximize your chances of success. In order to maximize the likelihood of success, you've got to prepare in advance. This means taking practice tests and spending time learning the information and test taking strategies you will need to succeed.

Never take the test as a "practice" test, expecting that you can just take it again if you need to. Feel free to take sample tests on your own, but when you go to take the official test, be prepared, be focused, and do your best the first time!

Secret Key #5 - Test Yourself

Everyone knows that time is money. There is no need to spend too much of your time or too little of your time preparing for the test. You should only spend as much of your precious time preparing as is necessary for you to get the score you need.

Once you have taken a practice test under real conditions of time constraints, then you will know if you are ready for the test or not.

If you have scored extremely high the first time that you take the practice test, then there is not much point in spending countless hours studying. You are already there.

Benchmark your abilities by retaking practice tests and seeing how much you have improved. Once you score high enough to guarantee success, then you are ready.

If you have scored well below where you need, then knuckle down and begin studying in earnest. Check your improvement regularly through the use of practice tests under real conditions. Above all, don't worry, panic, or give up. The key is perseverance!

Then, when you go to take the test, remain confident and remember how well you did on the practice tests. If you can score high enough on a practice test, then you can do the same on the real thing.

General Strategies

The most important thing you can do is to ignore your fears and jump into the test immediately- do not be overwhelmed by any strange-sounding terms. You have to jump into the test like jumping into a pool- all at once is the easiest way.

Make Predictions

As you read and understand the question, try to guess what the answer will be. Remember that several of the answer choices are wrong, and once you begin reading them, your mind will immediately become cluttered with answer choices designed to throw you off. Your mind is typically the most focused immediately after you have read the question and digested its contents. If you can, try to predict what the correct answer will be. You may be surprised at what you can predict.

Quickly scan the choices and see if your prediction is in the listed answer choices. If it is, then you can be quite confident that you have the right answer. It still won't hurt to check the other answer choices, but most of the time, you've got it!

Answer the Question

It may seem obvious to only pick answer choices that answer the question, but the test writers can create some excellent answer choices that are wrong. Don't pick an answer just because it sounds right, or you believe it to be true. It MUST answer the question. Once you've made your selection, always go back and check it against the question and make sure that you didn't misread the question, and the answer choice does answer the question posed.

Benchmark

After you read the first answer choice, decide if you think it sounds correct or not. If it doesn't, move on to the next answer choice. If it does, mentally mark that answer choice. This doesn't mean that you've definitely selected it as your answer choice, it just means that it's the best you've seen thus far. Go ahead and read the next choice. If the next choice is worse than the one you've already selected, keep going to the next answer choice. If the next choice is better than the choice you've already selected, mentally mark the new answer choice as your best guess.

The first answer choice that you select becomes your standard. Every other answer choice must be benchmarked against that standard. That choice is correct until proven otherwise by another answer choice beating it out. Once you've decided that no other answer choice seems as good, do one final check to ensure that your answer choice answers the question posed.

Valid Information

Don't discount any of the information provided in the question. Every piece of information may be necessary to determine the correct answer. None of the information in the question is there to throw you off (while the answer choices will certainly have information to throw you off). If two seemingly unrelated topics are discussed, don't ignore either. You can be confident there is a relationship, or it wouldn't be included in the question, and you are probably going to have to determine what is that relationship to find the answer.

Avoid "Fact Traps"

Don't get distracted by a choice that is factually true. Your search is for the answer that answers the question. Stay focused and don't fall for an answer that is true but incorrect. Always go back to the question and make sure you're choosing an answer that actually answers the question and is not just a true statement. An answer can be factually correct, but it MUST answer the question asked. Additionally, two answers can both be seemingly correct, so be sure to read all of the answer choices, and make sure that you get the one that BEST answers the question.

Milk the Question

Some of the questions may throw you completely off. They might deal with a

Copyright © Mometrix Media. You have been licensed one copy of this document for personal use only. Any other reproduction or distribution is strictly prohibited. All rights reserved.

subject you have not been exposed to, or one that you haven't reviewed in years. While your lack of knowledge about the subject will be a hindrance, the question itself can give you many clues that will help you find the correct answer. Read the question carefully and look for clues. Watch particularly for adjectives and nouns describing difficult terms or words that you don't recognize. Regardless of if you completely understand a word or not, replacing it with a synonym either provided or one you more familiar with may help you to understand what the questions are asking. Rather than wracking your mind about specific detailed information concerning a difficult term or word, try to use mental substitutes that are easier to understand.

The Trap of Familiarity

Don't just choose a word because you recognize it. On difficult questions, you may not recognize a number of words in the answer choices. The test writers don't put "make-believe" words on the test; so don't think that just because you only recognize all the words in one answer choice means that answer choice must be correct. If you only recognize words in one answer choice, then focus on that one. Is it correct? Try your best to determine if it is correct. If it is, that is great, but if it doesn't, eliminate it. Each word and answer choice you eliminate increases your chances of getting the question correct, even if you then have to guess among the unfamiliar choices.

Eliminate Answers

Eliminate choices as soon as you realize they are wrong. But be careful! Make sure you consider all of the possible answer choices. Just because one appears right, doesn't mean that the next one won't be even better! The test writers will usually put more than one good answer choice for every question, so read all of them. Don't worry if you are stuck between two that seem right. By getting down to just two remaining possible choices, your odds are now 50/50. Rather than wasting too much time, play the odds. You are guessing, but guessing wisely, because you've been able to knock out some of the answer choices that you know are wrong. If you are eliminating choices and realize that the last answer choice you are left with is also obviously wrong, don't panic. Start over and consider each choice again. There may easily be something that you missed the first time and will realize on the second pass.

Tough Questions

If you are stumped on a problem or it appears too hard or too difficult, don't waste time. Move on! Remember though, if you can quickly check for obviously incorrect answer choices, your chances of guessing correctly are greatly improved. Before you completely give up, at least try to knock out a couple of possible answers. Eliminate what you can and then guess at the remaining answer choices before moving on.

Brainstorm

If you get stuck on a difficult question, spend a few seconds quickly brainstorming. Run through the complete list of possible answer choices. Look at each choice and ask yourself, "Could this answer the question satisfactorily?" Go through each answer choice and consider it independently of the other. By systematically going through all possibilities, you may find something that you would otherwise overlook. Remember that when you get stuck, it's important to try to keep moving.

Read Carefully

Understand the problem. Read the question and answer choices carefully. Don't miss the question because you misread the terms. You have plenty of time to read each question thoroughly and make sure you understand what is being asked. Yet a happy medium must be attained, so don't waste too much time. You must read carefully, but efficiently.

Face Value

When in doubt, use common sense. Always accept the situation in the problem at face value. Don't read too much into it. These problems will not require you to make huge leaps of logic. The test writers aren't trying to throw you off with a cheap trick. If you have to go beyond creativity and make a leap of logic in order to have an answer choice answer the question, then you should look at the other answer choices. Don't overcomplicate the problem by creating theoretical relationships or explanations that will warp time or space. These are normal problems rooted in reality. It's just that the applicable relationship or explanation may not be readily apparent and you have to figure things out. Use your common sense to interpret anything that isn't clear.

Prefixes

If you're having trouble with a word in the question or answer choices, try dissecting it. Take advantage of every clue that the word might include. Prefixes and suffixes can be a huge help. Usually they allow you to determine a basic meaning. Pre- means before, post- means after, pro - is positive, de- is negative. From these prefixes and suffixes, you can get an idea of the general meaning of the word and try to put it into context. Beware though of any traps. Just because con is the opposite of pro, doesn't necessarily mean congress is the opposite of progress!

Hedge Phrases

Watch out for critical "hedge" phrases, such as likely, may, can, will often, sometimes, often, almost, mostly, usually, generally, rarely, sometimes. Question writers insert these hedge phrases to cover every possibility. Often an answer choice will be wrong simply because it leaves no room for exception. Avoid answer choices that have definitive words like "exactly," and "always".

Switchback Words

Stay alert for "switchbacks". These are the words and phrases frequently used to alert you to shifts in thought. The most common switchback word is "but". Others include although, however, nevertheless, on the other hand, even though, while, in spite of, despite, regardless of.

New Information

Correct answer choices will rarely have completely new information included. Answer choices typically are straightforward reflections of the material asked about and will directly relate to the question. If a new piece of information is included in an answer choice that doesn't even seem to relate to the topic being asked about, then that answer choice is likely incorrect. All of the information needed to answer the question is usually provided for you, and so you should not have to make guesses that are unsupported or choose answer choices that require unknown information that cannot be reasoned on its own.

Time Management

On technical questions, don't get lost on the technical terms. Don't spend too much time on any one question. If you don't know what a term means, then since you don't have a dictionary, odds are you aren't going to get much further. You should immediately recognize terms as whether or not you know them. If you don't, work with the other clues that you have, the other answer choices and terms provided, but don't waste too much time trying to figure out a difficult term.

Contextual Clues

Look for contextual clues. An answer can be right but not correct. The contextual clues will help you find the answer that is most right and is correct. Understand the context in which a phrase or statement is made. This will help you make important distinctions.

Don't Panic

Panicking will not answer any questions for you. Therefore, it isn't helpful. When you first see the question, if your mind goes blank, take a deep breath. Force yourself to mechanically go through the steps of solving the problem and using the strategies you've learned.

Pace Yourself

Don't get clock fever. It's easy to be overwhelmed when you're looking at a page full of questions, your mind is full of random thoughts and feeling confused, and the clock is ticking down faster than you would like. Calm down and maintain the pace that you have set for yourself. As long as you are on track by monitoring your pace, you are guaranteed to have enough time for yourself. When you get to the last few minutes of the test, it may seem like you won't have enough time left, but if you only have as many questions as you should have left at that point, then you're right on track!

Answer Selection

The best way to pick an answer choice is to eliminate all of those that are wrong, until only one is left and confirm that is the correct answer. Sometimes though, an answer choice may immediately look right. Be careful! Take a second to make sure that the other choices are not equally obvious. Don't make a hasty mistake. There are only two times that you should stop before checking other answers. First is when you are positive that the answer choice you have selected is correct. Second is when time is almost out and you have to make a quick guess!

Check Your Work

Since you will probably not know every term listed and the answer to every question, it is important that you get credit for the ones that you do know. Don't miss any questions through careless mistakes. If at all possible, try to take a second to look back over your answer selection and make sure you've selected the correct answer choice and haven't made a costly careless mistake (such as marking an answer choice that you didn't mean to mark). This quick double check should more than pay for itself in caught mistakes for the time it costs.

Beware of Directly Quoted Answers

Sometimes an answer choice will repeat word for word a portion of the question or reference section. However, beware of such exact duplication – it may be a trap! More than likely, the correct choice will paraphrase or summarize a point, rather than being exactly the same wording.

Slang

Scientific sounding answers are better than slang ones. An answer choice that begins "To compare the outcomes…" is much more likely to be correct than one that begins "Because some people insisted…"

Extreme Statements

Avoid wild answers that throw out highly controversial ideas that are proclaimed as established fact. An answer choice that states the "process should be used in certain situations, if…" is much more likely to be correct than one that states the "process should be discontinued completely."   The first is a calm rational statement and doesn't even make a definitive, uncompromising stance, using a hedge word "if" to provide wiggle room, whereas the second choice is a radical idea and far more extreme.

Answer Choice Families

When you have two or more answer choices that are direct opposites or parallels, one of them is usually the correct answer. For instance, if one answer choice states "x increases" and another answer choice states "x decreases" or "y increases," then those two or three answer choices are very similar in construction and fall into the same family of answer choices. A family of answer choices is when two or three answer choices are very similar in construction, and yet often have a directly opposite meaning. Usually the correct answer choice will be in that family of answer choices. The "odd man out" or answer choice that doesn't seem to fit the parallel construction of the other answer choices is more likely to be incorrect.

Special Report: What Your Test Score Will Tell You About Your IQ

Did you know that most standardized tests correlate very strongly with IQ? In fact, your general intelligence is a better predictor of your success than any other factor, and most tests intentionally measure this trait to some degree to ensure that those selected by the test are truly qualified for the test's purposes.

Before we can delve into the relation between your test score and IQ, I will first have to explain what exactly is IQ. Here's the formula:

Your IQ = 100 + (Number of standard deviations below or above the average)*15

Now, let's define standard deviations by using an example. If we have 5 people with 5 different heights, then first we calculate the average. Let's say the average was 65 inches. The standard deviation is the "average distance" away from the average of each of the members. It is a direct measure of variability - if the 5 people included Jackie Chan and Shaquille O'Neal, obviously there's a lot more variability in that group than a group of 5 sisters who are all within 6 inches in height of each other. The standard deviation uses a number to characterize the average range of difference within a group.

A convenient feature of most groups is that they have a "normal" distribution- makes sense that most things would be normal, right? Without getting into a bunch of statistical mumbo-jumbo, you just need to know that if you know the average of the group and the standard deviation, you can successfully predict someone's percentile rank in the group.

Confused? Let me give you an example. If instead of 5 people's heights, we had 100 people, we could figure out their rank in height JUST by knowing the average, standard deviation, and their height. We wouldn't need to know each person's height and manually rank them, we could just predict their rank based on three numbers.

What this means is that you can take your PERCENTILE rank that is often given with your test and relate this to your RELATIVE IQ of people taking the test - that is, your IQ relative to the people taking the test. Obviously, there's no way to know your actual IQ because the people taking a standardized test are usually not very good samples of the general population- many of those with extremely low IQ's never achieve a level of success or competency necessary to complete a typical standardized test. In fact, professional psychologists who measure IQ actually have to use non-written tests that can fairly measure the IQ of those not able to complete a traditional test.

The bottom line is to not take your test score too seriously, but it is fun to compute your "relative IQ" among the people who took the test with you. I've done the calculations below. Just look up your percentile rank in the left and then you'll see your "relative IQ" for your test in the right hand column-

Percentile Rank	Your Relative IQ		Percentile Rank	Your Relative IQ
99	135		59	103
98	131		58	103
97	128		57	103
96	126		56	102
95	125		55	102
94	123		54	102
93	122		53	101
92	121		52	101
91	120		51	100
90	119		50	100
89	118		49	100
88	118		48	99
87	117		47	99
86	116		46	98
85	116		45	98
84	115		44	98
83	114		43	97
82	114		42	97
81	113		41	97
80	113		40	96
79	112		39	96
78	112		38	95
77	111		37	95
76	111		36	95
75	110		35	94
74	110		34	94
73	109		33	93
72	109		32	93
71	108		31	93
70	108		30	92
69	107		29	92
68	107		28	91
67	107		27	91
66	106		26	90
65	106		25	90
64	105		24	89
63	105		23	89
62	105		22	88
61	104		21	88
60	104		20	87

Special Report: What is Test Anxiety and How to Overcome It?

The very nature of tests caters to some level of anxiety, nervousness or tension, just as we feel for any important event that occurs in our lives. A little bit of anxiety or nervousness can be a good thing. It helps us with motivation, and makes achievement just that much sweeter. However, too much anxiety can be a problem; especially if it hinders our ability to function and perform.

"Test anxiety," is the term that refers to the emotional reactions that some test-takers experience when faced with a test or exam. Having a fear of testing and exams is based upon a rational fear, since the test-taker's performance can shape the course of an academic career. Nevertheless, experiencing excessive fear of examinations will only interfere with the test-takers ability to perform, and his/her chances to be successful.

There are a large variety of causes that can contribute to the development and sensation of test anxiety. These include, but are not limited to lack of performance and worrying about issues surrounding the test.

Lack of Preparation

Lack of preparation can be identified by the following behaviors or situations:

Not scheduling enough time to study, and therefore cramming the night before the test or exam
Managing time poorly, to create the sensation that there is not enough time to do everything

Failing to organize the text information in advance, so that the study material consists of the entire text and not simply the pertinent information

Poor overall studying habits

Worrying, on the other hand, can be related to both the test taker, or many other factors around him/her that will be affected by the results of the test. These include worrying about:

Previous performances on similar exams, or exams in general

How friends and other students are achieving

The negative consequences that will result from a poor grade or failure

There are three primary elements to test anxiety. Physical components, which involve the same typical bodily reactions as those to acute anxiety (to be discussed below). Emotional factors have to do with fear or panic. Mental or cognitive issues concerning attention spans and memory abilities.

Physical Signals

There are many different symptoms of test anxiety, and these are not limited to mental and emotional strain. Frequently there are a range of physical signals that will let a test taker know that he/she is suffering from test anxiety. These bodily changes can include the following:

Perspiring

Sweaty palms

Wet, trembling hands

Nausea

Dry mouth

A knot in the stomach

Headache

Faintness

Muscle tension

Aching shoulders, back and neck

Rapid heart beat

Feeling too hot/cold

To recognize the sensation of test anxiety, a test-taker should monitor him/herself for the following sensations:

The physical distress symptoms as listed above

Emotional sensitivity, expressing emotional feelings such as the need to cry or laugh too much, or a sensation of anger or helplessness

A decreased ability to think, causing the test-taker to blank out or have racing thoughts that are hard to organize or control.

Though most students will feel some level of anxiety when faced with a test or exam, the majority can cope with that anxiety and maintain it at a manageable level. However, those who cannot are faced with a very real and very serious condition, which can and should be controlled for the immeasurable benefit of this sufferer.

Naturally, these sensations lead to negative results for the testing experience. The most common effects of test anxiety have to do with nervousness and mental blocking.

Nervousness

Nervousness can appear in several different levels:

The test-taker's difficulty, or even inability to read and understand the questions on the test

The difficulty or inability to organize thoughts to a coherent form

The difficulty or inability to recall key words and concepts relating to the testing questions (especially essays)

The receipt of poor grades on a test, though the test material was well known by the test taker

Conversely, a person may also experience mental blocking, which involves:

Blanking out on test questions

Only remembering the correct answers to the questions when the test has already finished.

Fortunately for test anxiety sufferers, beating these feelings, to a large degree, has to do with proper preparation. When a test taker has a feeling of preparedness, then anxiety will be dramatically lessened.

The first step to resolving anxiety issues is to distinguish which of the two types of anxiety are being suffered. If the anxiety is a direct result of a lack of preparation, this should be considered a normal reaction, and the anxiety level (as opposed to the test results) shouldn't be anything to worry about. However, if, when adequately prepared, the test-taker still panics, blanks out, or seems to overreact, this is not a fully rational reaction. While this can be considered normal too, there are many ways to combat and overcome these effects.

Remember that anxiety cannot be entirely eliminated, however, there are ways to minimize it, to make the anxiety easier to manage. Preparation is one of the best ways to minimize test anxiety. Therefore the following techniques are wise in order to best fight off any anxiety that may want to build.

To begin with, try to avoid cramming before a test, whenever it is possible. By trying to memorize an entire term's worth of information in one day, you'll be shocking your system, and not giving yourself a very good chance to absorb the information. This is an easy path to anxiety, so for those who suffer from test anxiety, cramming should not even be considered an option.

Instead of cramming, work throughout the semester to combine all of the material which is presented throughout the semester, and work on it gradually as the course goes by, making sure to master the main concepts first, leaving minor details for a week or so before the test.

To study for the upcoming exam, be sure to pose questions that may be on the examination, to gauge the ability to answer them by integrating the ideas from your texts, notes and lectures, as well as any supplementary readings.

If it is truly impossible to cover all of the information that was covered in that particular term, concentrate on the most important portions, that can be covered very well. Learn these concepts as best as possible, so that when the test comes, a goal can be made to use these concepts as presentations of your knowledge.

In addition to study habits, changes in attitude are critical to beating a struggle with test anxiety. In fact, an improvement of the perspective over the entire test-taking experience can actually help a test taker to enjoy studying and therefore improve the overall experience. Be certain not to overemphasize the significance of the grade - know that the result of the test is neither a reflection of self worth, nor is it a measure of intelligence; one grade will not predict a person's future success.

To improve an overall testing outlook, the following steps should be tried:

Keeping in mind that the most reasonable expectation for taking a test is to expect to try to demonstrate as much of what you know as you possibly can. Reminding ourselves that a test is only one test; this is not the only one, and there will be others.

The thought of thinking of oneself in an irrational, all-or-nothing term should be avoided at all costs.

A reward should be designated for after the test, so there's something to look forward to. Whether it be going to a movie, going out to eat, or simply visiting friends, schedule it in advance, and do it no matter what result is expected on the exam.

Test-takers should also keep in mind that the basics are some of the most important things, even beyond anti-anxiety techniques and studying. Never neglect the basic social, emotional and biological needs, in order to try to absorb information. In order to best achieve, these three factors must be held as just as important as the studying itself.

Study Steps

Remember the following important steps for studying:

Maintain healthy nutrition and exercise habits. Continue both your recreational activities and social pass times. These both contribute to your physical and emotional well being.

Be certain to get a good amount of sleep, especially the night before the test, because when you're overtired you are not able to perform to the best of your best ability.

Keep the studying pace to a moderate level by taking breaks when they are needed, and varying the work whenever possible, to keep the mind fresh instead of getting bored.

When enough studying has been done that all the material that can be learned has been learned, and the test taker is prepared for the test, stop studying and do something relaxing such as listening to music, watching a movie, or taking a warm bubble bath.

There are also many other techniques to minimize the uneasiness or apprehension that is experienced along with test anxiety before, during, or even after the examination. In fact, there are a great deal of things that can be done to stop anxiety from interfering with lifestyle and performance. Again, remember that anxiety will not be eliminated entirely, and it shouldn't be. Otherwise that "up" feeling for exams would not exist, and most of us depend on that sensation to perform better than usual. However, this anxiety has to be at a level that is manageable.

Of course, as we have just discussed, being prepared for the exam is half the battle right away. Attending all classes, finding out what knowledge will be expected on the exam, and knowing the exam schedules are easy steps to lowering anxiety. Keeping up with work will remove the need to cram, and efficient study habits will eliminate wasted time. Studying should be done in an ideal location for concentration, so that it is simple to become interested in the material and give it complete attention. A method such as SQ3R (Survey, Question, Read, Recite, Review) is a wonderful key to follow to make sure that the study habits are as effective as possible, especially in the case of learning from a textbook. Flashcards are great techniques for memorization. Learning to take good notes will mean that notes will be full of useful information, so that less sifting will need to be done to seek out what is pertinent for studying. Reviewing notes after class and then again on occasion will keep the information fresh in the mind. From notes that have been taken summary sheets and outlines can be made for simpler reviewing.

A study group can also be a very motivational and helpful place to study, as there will be a sharing of ideas, all of the minds can work together, to make sure that everyone understands, and the studying will be made more interesting because it will be a social occasion.

Basically, though, as long as the test-taker remains organized and self confident, with efficient study habits, less time will need to be spent studying, and higher grades will be achieved.

To become self confident, there are many useful steps. The first of these is "self talk." It has been shown through extensive research, that self-talk for students who suffer from test anxiety, should be well monitored, in order to make sure that it contributes to self confidence as opposed to sinking the student. Frequently the self talk of test-anxious students is negative or self-defeating, thinking that everyone else is smarter and faster, that they always mess up, and that if they don't do well, they'll fail the entire course. It is important to decreasing anxiety that awareness is made of self talk. Try writing any negative self thoughts and then disputing them with a positive statement instead. Begin self-encouragement as though it was a friend speaking. Repeat positive statements to help reprogram the mind to believing in successes instead of failures.

Helpful Techniques

Other extremely helpful techniques include:

Self-visualization of doing well and reaching goals

While aiming for an "A" level of understanding, don't try to "overprotect" by setting your expectations lower. This will only convince the mind to stop studying in order to meet the lower expectations.

Don't make comparisons with the results or habits of other students. These are individual factors, and different things work for different people, causing different results.

Strive to become an expert in learning what works well, and what can be done in order to improve. Consider collecting this data in a journal.

Create rewards for after studying instead of doing things before studying that will only turn into avoidance behaviors.

Make a practice of relaxing - by using methods such as progressive relaxation, self-hypnosis, guided imagery, etc - in order to make relaxation an automatic sensation.

Work on creating a state of relaxed concentration so that concentrating will take on the focus of the mind, so that none will be wasted on worrying.

Take good care of the physical self by eating well and getting enough sleep.

Plan in time for exercise and stick to this plan.

Beyond these techniques, there are other methods to be used before, during and after the test that will help the test-taker perform well in addition to overcoming anxiety.

Before the exam comes the academic preparation. This involves establishing a study schedule and beginning at least one week before the actual date of the test. By doing this, the anxiety of not having enough time to study for the test will be automatically eliminated. Moreover, this will make the studying a much more effective experience, ensuring that the learning will be an easier process. This relieves much undue pressure on the test-taker.

Summary sheets, note cards, and flash cards with the main concepts and examples of these main concepts should be prepared in advance of the actual studying time. A topic should never be eliminated from this process. By omitting a topic because it isn't expected to be on the test is only setting up the test-taker for anxiety should it actually appear on the exam. Utilize the course syllabus for laying out the topics that should be studied. Carefully go over the notes that were made in class, paying special attention to any of the issues that the professor took special care to emphasize while lecturing in class. In the textbooks, use the chapter review, or if possible, the chapter tests, to begin your review.

It may even be possible to ask the instructor what information will be covered on the exam, or what the format of the exam will be (for example, multiple choice, essay, free form, true-false). Additionally, see if it is possible to find out how many questions will be on the test. If a review sheet or sample test has been offered by the professor, make good use of it, above anything else, for the preparation for the test. Another great resource for getting to know the examination is reviewing tests from previous semesters. Use these tests to review, and aim to achieve a 100% score on each of the possible topics. With a few exceptions, the goal that you set for yourself is the highest one that you will reach.

Take all of the questions that were assigned as homework, and rework them to any other possible course material. The more problems reworked, the more skill and confidence will form as a result. When forming the solution to a problem, write out each of the steps. Don't simply do head work. By doing as many steps on paper as possible, much clarification and therefore confidence will be formed. Do this with as many homework problems as possible, before checking the answers. By checking the answer after each problem, a reinforcement will exist, that will not be on the exam. Study situations should be as exam-like as possible, to prime the test-taker's system for the experience. By waiting to check the answers at the end, a psychological advantage will be formed, to decrease the stress factor.

Another fantastic reason for not cramming is the avoidance of confusion in concepts, especially when it comes to mathematics. 8-10 hours of study will become one hundred percent more effective if it is spread out over a week or at least several days, instead of doing it all in one sitting. Recognize that the human brain requires time in order to assimilate new material, so frequent breaks and a span of study time over several days will be much more beneficial.

Additionally, don't study right up until the point of the exam. Studying should stop a minimum of one hour before the exam begins. This allows the brain to rest and put things in their proper order. This will also provide the time to become as relaxed as possible when going into the examination room. The test-taker will also have time to eat well and eat sensibly. Know that the brain needs food as much as the rest of the body. With enough food and enough sleep, as well as a relaxed attitude, the body and the mind are primed for success.

Avoid any anxious classmates who are talking about the exam. These students only spread anxiety, and are not worth sharing the anxious sentimentalities.

Before the test also involves creating a positive attitude, so mental preparation should also be a point of concentration. There are many keys to creating a positive attitude. Should fears become rushing in, make a visualization of taking the exam, doing well, and seeing an A written on the paper. Write out a list of affirmations that will bring a feeling of confidence, such as "I am doing well in my English class," "I studied well and know my material," "I enjoy this class." Even if the affirmations aren't believed at first, it sends a positive message to the subconscious which will result in an alteration of the overall belief system, which is the system that creates reality.

If a sensation of panic begins, work with the fear and imagine the very worst! Work through the entire scenario of not passing the test, failing the entire course, and dropping out of school, followed by not getting a job, and pushing a shopping cart through the dark alley where you'll live. This will place things into perspective! Then, practice deep breathing and create a visualization of the opposite situation - achieving an "A" on the exam, passing the entire course, receiving the degree at a graduation ceremony.

On the day of the test, there are many things to be done to ensure the best results, as well as the most calm outlook. The following stages are suggested in order to maximize test-taking potential:

Begin the examination day with a moderate breakfast, and avoid any coffee or beverages with caffeine if the test taker is prone to jitters. Even people who are used to managing caffeine can feel jittery or light-headed when it is taken on a test day.

Attempt to do something that is relaxing before the examination begins. As last minute cramming clouds the mastering of overall concepts, it is better to use this time to create a calming outlook.

Be certain to arrive at the test location well in advance, in order to provide time to select a location that is away from doors, windows and other distractions, as well as giving enough time to relax before the test begins.

Keep away from anxiety generating classmates who will upset the sensation of stability and relaxation that is being attempted before the exam.

Should the waiting period before the exam begins cause anxiety, create a self-distraction by reading a light magazine or something else that is relaxing and simple.

During the exam itself, read the entire exam from beginning to end, and find out how much time should be allotted to each individual problem. Once writing the exam, should more time be taken for a problem, it should be abandoned, in order to begin another problem. If there is time at the end, the unfinished problem can always be returned to and completed.

Read the instructions very carefully - twice - so that unpleasant surprises won't follow during or after the exam has ended.

When writing the exam, pretend that the situation is actually simply the completion of homework within a library, or at home. This will assist in forming a relaxed atmosphere, and will allow the brain extra focus for the complex thinking function.

Begin the exam with all of the questions with which the most confidence is felt. This will build the confidence level regarding the entire exam and will begin a quality momentum. This will also create encouragement for trying the problems where uncertainty resides.

Going with the "gut instinct" is always the way to go when solving a problem. Second guessing should be avoided at all costs. Have confidence in the ability to do well.

For essay questions, create an outline in advance that will keep the mind organized and make certain that all of the points are remembered. For multiple choice, read every answer, even if the correct one has been spotted - a better one may exist.

Continue at a pace that is reasonable and not rushed, in order to be able to work carefully. Provide enough time to go over the answers at the end, to check for small errors that can be corrected.

Should a feeling of panic begin, breathe deeply, and think of the feeling of the body releasing sand through its pores. Visualize a calm, peaceful place, and include all of the sights, sounds and sensations of this image. Continue the deep breathing, and take a few minutes to continue this with closed eyes. When all is well again, return to the test.

If a "blanking" occurs for a certain question, skip it and move on to the next question. There will be time to return to the other question later. Get everything done that can be done, first, to guarantee all the grades that can be compiled, and to build all of the confidence possible. Then return to the weaker questions to build the marks from there.

Remember, one's own reality can be created, so as long as the belief is there, success will follow. And remember: anxiety can happen later, right now, there's an exam to be written!

After the examination is complete, whether there is a feeling for a good grade or a bad grade, don't dwell on the exam, and be certain to follow through on the reward that was promised...and enjoy it! Don't dwell on any mistakes that have been made, as there is nothing that can be done at this point anyway.

Additionally, don't begin to study for the next test right away. Do something relaxing for a while, and let the mind relax and prepare itself to begin absorbing information again.

From the results of the exam - both the grade and the entire experience, be certain to learn from what has gone on. Perfect studying habits and work some more on confidence in order to make the next examination experience even better than the last one.

Learn to avoid places where openings occurred for laziness, procrastination and day dreaming.

Use the time between this exam and the next one to better learn to relax, even learning to relax on cue, so that any anxiety can be controlled during the next exam. Learn how to relax the body. Slouch in your chair if that helps. Tighten and then relax all of the different muscle groups, one group at a time, beginning with the feet and then working all the way up to the neck and face. This will ultimately relax the muscles more than they were to begin with. Learn how to breathe deeply and comfortably, and focus on this breathing going in and out as a relaxing thought. With every exhale, repeat the word "relax."

As common as test anxiety is, it is very possible to overcome it. Make yourself one of the test-takers who overcome this frustrating hindrance.

Special Report: Retaking the Test: What Are Your Chances at Improving Your Score?

After going through the experience of taking a major test, many test takers feel that once is enough. The test usually comes during a period of transition in the test taker's life, and taking the test is only one of a series of important events. With so many distractions and conflicting recommendations, it may be difficult for a test taker to rationally determine whether or not he should retake the test after viewing his scores.

The importance of the test usually only adds to the burden of the retake decision. However, don't be swayed by emotion. There a few simple questions that you can ask yourself to guide you as you try to determine whether a retake would improve your score:

1. What went wrong? Why wasn't your score what you expected?

Can you point to a single factor or problem that you feel caused the low score? Were you sick on test day? Was there an emotional upheaval in your life that caused a distraction? Were you late for the test or not able to use the full time allotment? If you can point to any of these specific, individual problems, then a retake should definitely be considered.

2. Is there enough time to improve?

Many problems that may show up in your score report may take a lot of time for improvement. A deficiency in a particular math skill may require weeks or months of tutoring and studying to improve. If you have enough time to improve an identified weakness, then a retake should definitely be considered.

3. How will additional scores be used? Will a score average, highest score, or most recent score be used?

Different test scores may be handled completely differently. If you've taken the test multiple times, sometimes your highest score is used, sometimes your average score is computed and used, and sometimes your most recent score is used. Make sure you understand what method will be used to evaluate your scores, and use that to help you determine whether a retake should be considered.

4. Are my practice test scores significantly higher than my actual test score?

If you have taken a lot of practice tests and are consistently scoring at a much higher level than your actual test score, then you should consider a retake. However, if you've taken five practice tests and only one of your scores was higher than your actual test score, or if your practice test scores were only slightly higher than your actual test score, then it is unlikely that you will significantly increase your score.

5. Do I need perfect scores or will I be able to live with this score? Will this score still allow me to follow my dreams?

What kind of score is acceptable to you? Is your current score "good enough?" Do you have to have a certain score in order to pursue the future of your dreams? If you won't be happy with your current score, and there's no way that you could live with it, then you should consider a retake. However, don't get your hopes up. If you are looking for significant improvement, that may or may not be possible. But if you won't be happy otherwise, it is at least worth the effort.

Remember that there are other considerations. To achieve your dream, it is likely that your grades may also be taken into account. A great test score is usually not the only thing necessary to succeed. Make sure that you aren't overemphasizing the importance of a high test score.

Furthermore, a retake does not always result in a higher score. Some test takers will score lower on a retake, rather than higher. One study shows that one-fourth of test takers will achieve a significant improvement in test score, while one-sixth of test takers will actually show a decrease. While this shows that most test takers will improve, the majority will only improve their scores a little and a retake may not be worth the test taker's effort.

Finally, if a test is taken only once and is considered in the added context of good grades on the part of a test taker, the person reviewing the grades and scores may be tempted to assume that the test taker just had a bad day while taking the test, and may discount the low test score in favor of the high grades. But if the test is retaken and the scores are approximately the same, then the validity of the low scores are only confirmed. Therefore, a retake could actually hurt a test taker by definitely bracketing a test taker's score ability to a limited range.